Breathing Words
A Year of Writing Together

Kathy,

    I have been fortunate enough to have so many strong mothers in my life. I'm so grateful you are one of them.

        I love you,

        Whitney

Breathing Words
A Year of Writing Together

Set in Palatino and Gill Sans
Cover design: Phil Saltonstall, www.philsaltonstall.com
Interior design: Leslie I. Bolin, www.studiosouthpaw.com

Printed in the United States of America

ISBN-10:0-9990894-0-4

Contents

Introduction

In the summer of 2015, a group of thousands of writers enrolled in a thirty-day writing challenge founded by Andréa Balt called Write Yourself Alive! The title attracted many of us from around the world who were inspired to change our lives through writing. At the first prompt of the first day, most of us hesitated, our index finger hovering over the enter key. Many of us were about to expose our writing to thousands of strangers for the first time. We held our breath, hit the key, and magic began to happen.

Comments on our posts began to flow. Other writers offered constructive feedback and encouragement mingled with genuine concern for the emotions we revealed. We looked forward each day to challenging ourselves in this safe environment. We opened our souls to each other, sharing our personal stories, connecting in genuine and deep ways. This was social media as it was intended to be, a tool for creating true relationships with people we might never have met. Here we were free to be ourselves. We began to breathe again.

It quickly became clear that certain members of the group read and commented on almost every post. We gravitated to each other, drawn by the commonality of the open and empathic personality. By the end of the thirty days, strong bonds had formed that we couldn't bear to see end. On the last day we decided to hold a prom. We played "Dancing in the Moonlight" on our mobile phones and computers and danced alone together under the light of a full summer moon.

We continued to write in a newly formed group of approximately one hundred members over the following year. This diverse group of the widowed and abused, the conservative and the liberal, the atheist and the religious, the business person and the unemployed, the musician and the actress, the gay and straight all came together in a unified voice. Our styles varied greatly and our differences were celebrated. Here, the only rule was love and kindness. Judgment was checked at the door.

One of our members who had never written a poem before began to flourish. Her book of poems was published successfully. Her work was featured in The Galway Literary Review in Ireland. The rest of us were inspired by her success. Others began to be published and create writer pages with tens of thousands of followers collectively. Our words born in this crucible began to turn to the outside world as we healed. We began to feel the inevitable shift of focus from the comfort of our group to one of individual purpose. Before we moved any further, we knew the world should hear our story.

The idea of publishing an anthology together rose and died and rose again. After much discussion and a little angst we created a framework. The format was simple; five pieces each, no rules. Whoever wanted to contribute would be accepted. Everyone could play a part. Some stepped up as editors, others as organizers and designers. This book is the result.

The title was a natural choice. Breath is synonymous with life. Through our journey together, we came alive in new ways. We closed the space between us with words, with breath. Our inspiration and exhalation of shared words in this closed room moved us to deep inner spaces. We laughed, wept, prayed, and breathed a million words.

A few of us did finally meet in person. One small group met at Vesuvio Café in San Francisco and across the alley at City Lights Bookstore. There among the ghosts of the Beat poets they wrote poetry together and passed out notebooks to strangers who wrote with them. Another member travelled across the country threading many of us together in a series of meetings as we all followed his journey in posts. Perhaps we will all meet one day as a culmination of this experience. We talk of it often, though we all agree our connections could not be deeper.

Somewhere among us is The Traveling Box of the Poet's Heart. This mysterious box magically appears on a member's doorstep. A hand-made gift is added and the box travels on to the next member. The items are secret delights, offerings from the collected hearts of friends. It is overwhelming to hold these physical symbols created by love.

It is our sincere hope you find inspiration here for your personal journey. Join us around the fire as we tell our stories. This is a work of love.

IT'S HERE...AROUND THIS FIRE

Joel Usher
Transcribed by Steven Hashimoto

Watch Joel Usher perform the song: https://youtu.be/rq4D5vR7-G0

Charts by Hashimoto (708) 660-9469

2   IT'S HERE...AROUND THIS FIRE

IT'S HERE...AROUND THIS FIRE 3

4

IT'S HERE...AROUND THIS FIRE

IT'S HERE...AROUND THIS FIRE

5

6   IT'S HERE...AROUND THIS FIRE

IT'S HERE...AROUND THIS FIRE

7

8   IT'S HERE...AROUND THIS FIRE

IT'S HERE...AROUND THIS FIRE   9

shame the pain the blame we feel to - night   we leave here   in this

fire_____   for me and you   and you   and you   Oh all the

shame the blame the pain we   feel to - night   we leave here   in this

10   IT'S HERE...AROUND THIS FIRE

fire   for me and you   and you   and you   for me and

you   and you and   you   for me and

you   and you and   you_____

Rachel Ballantine

My mother said that when I was two I was filling pages with handwriting. I have thirty feet of journals. I can't not write. I write poems, little essays, journals. I have written and published a book of poetry, "Still Fruit With Life" and "Recipoetry of a Kitchen Mystic." I wrote a paper on "This is a Sound Based Universe" which was published and translated into Korean and published through the international symposium of shamans. I studied writing with Natalie Goldberg when she was first doing her writing groups in Santa Fe. I have taught writing groups for many years. I am currently working on a book about the divine feminine. I am also a healer, massage therapist, artist, elder care helper, was a waitress for years. I am an award-winning book artist. I am interested in people, writing, reading, the world. I go for long walks and take my camera, note cards and a pen. I am embarking on a new year-long independent study of herbs to be a master herbalist. I have two cats and four birds and a huge Dodge truck. I live in Albuquerque and long for my home state of New York but am trying to make friends with the desert. I am published in several issues of The Malpais Review. But really, I want to be a good writer. Visit rachelsbooks.com; www.facebook.com/rachelsbooksnm. Love, Rachel.

© Rachel Ballantine

Winston, New Mexico

Where cowboy's skin
becomes like the land,
and the land and sky become hooves and barking.
Cowgirls don't examine their psyches—
they make potato salad
and ride horses the color of dirt.

Henry's grandfather bought
his grandmother for two horses.
He was 52; she was 19.
When the bells rang in town for a dance,
she didn't know they tolled
for her own wedding.

Henry couldn't find his bull for six months.
We found him yesterday; he had a hurt leg.
He was so big and black, like a thunderstorm.
I left him my apple on a fence post.
I hope he liked it.

The cowboys built a fire in a pit
and buried meat in a cast iron pot
for three days.
This was down the road
from where Bud Olsen lived
before he got shot for fooling around
with someone else's wife.

The squirrels live in the roof of the ranch house;
the swallows live on the porch.
The calves scream at their branding.
They fight for their nuts, but they lose.
Their tails drip with blood.

The kerosene lamps become dusty,
and the coyote puppies whisper and cry the sun up.
The old people built their houses out of the dirt,
and now the land is claiming those houses back,
pulling the adobe bricks down into herself.

Thunderstorms claim the valleys for their own
and leave behind swirling scars with tires and rusty cars.
The heels of the cowboy's boots look like hooves,
and there are homesteads hidden in the mountains
with cast iron cook stoves.
Nobody knows how they got them back there.

The Hungry Therapist

She was hungry for my story,
ravenous in fact, as if the story was
a dark cake.
She ate the secrets and hurts
that made her black eyes glisten,
and her long hair go wild.
The more I fed her
thick, rich crumbs
the hungrier she got,
and I could not keep the cake from her.
But then, on my birthday, she made ME a cake,
thick and dark,
and would not let me have any.
There will be no celebration today she said.
So I stopped feeding her my cake
of dark secrets.
She will have to find her black sugar
in somebody else's past.

Portrait

Down a dirt road she walked until the critters chirped their evening songs that faded into another dying day, leaving a rosy blue hum just over the mountains.

She walked into the night like it was a cellar, her feet orbits of pain and movement, no guiding light—inner or outer. She had become walking.

Something scurried next to her. She cried out, breaking the spell, and as she did, she saw a light, a tiny glimmer, barely pulsing against the dark waves of night. Her walk became broken and hurried until she came to a cabin that glowed like a jack-o-lantern through its windows and open front door.

Inside sat a man at a table eating soup from an earthen bowl. A cat lay on the table, not watching him but aware of his eating. In one corner was a fireplace and in the other corner was an easel. On the easel sat an unfinished painting, a portrait in infinite shades of blue.

It was a portrait of her.

He looked up.

He smiled.

He drew her in and washed her feet.

Neither of them spoke.

Things That Rust

In South Carolina, things rusted that didn't even have any metal content. Things like chocolate, cardboard, and plastic. It was a state of constant, continual active disintegration. My jewelry tools, my toolbox, my car, the hinges on my hair clip, my earring wires, the lids to jars, the refrigerator—everything rusted, molded, and sweated.

Decay was the current paradigm. The past lingered, forever in the present, taking over in the myriad forms of persistent rust that pounced on every non-living surface. Rust was a mouth with no body, chewing jagged holes in the underbellies of cars and the vulnerable surfaces of hammerheads and nails in walls.

Rust was an active life force, riding in on the salty ocean, the visible traitor of future shines.

If Not For You

If not for your hands,
God could not touch the cheek
of the beloved.
If not for your nose,
God could not smell peanut butter cookies baking,
roses, or the top of a baby's head.
If not for your eyes,
God could not see purple sunsets,
a weed, or the gleam of silver by candlelight.
If not for your feet,
God could not walk upon this
sweet earth.
If not for your loving,
God could not create the world
over and over again.

Susan Boardman

Hypnotherapy. Quilts. Newfoundland dogs. Kenzie. Gardens. Sticks & String. Change. The occasional sermon. Poems, oddly. Dr. Sue Boardman, Author. Artist. Activist. Grandmother. *Grandmothers Are In Charge Of Hope. We Gather Together...holiday feasts with the family you have! Let's Boil Bones...Grammy's guide to bone broth and other yummy things!* (Bestsellers!) Taylor. Color. Workshops. Contemplations. Grammy Camp. Teacher. **sueboardman.guru** Inspirational Speaker. Questions that make all the difference.

Facebook: www.facebook.com/sueboardman.guru

Grandmothers Lament

All over the world, children are crying.
Bleeding children in Syria.
Hurricane victims in Haiti.
Poisoned children in Michigan and the Dakotas and
too many places to count.
All over the world, children are crying.
Children robbed of their families by gun violence.
Children robbed of their futures by disease.
Children robbed of their health by toxins everywhere.
All over the world, children are crying.
How do we shut out their cries?
How do we not act?
Are we heartless?
All over the world, children are crying.
We who do care are helpless in many ways.
Rendered voiceless by the power of vested self
interest.
The power of greed.
All over the world, children are crying.
Hungry children.
Homeless children.
Abused, molested, victimized children.
All over the world, children are crying.
It is not our own greed that renders us helpless.
At least not mostly.
And yet we shout, silently, in the face of those who
love power.

All over the world, children are crying.
While the mighty grow rich waging war.
While the mighty grow rich selling power.
While the mighty grow rich killing the Earth.
All over the world, children are crying.
Let us take our fingers out of our ears.
Let us open our eyes in the light of day.
Let us shout until we cannot be ignored.
All over the world, children are crying.
Let us dare to hear.
Let us dare to hope.
Let us dare to act.
Amen. Amen. Selah.

(Untitled)

Moving, shifting, always changing ... fuzzy, tattered snapshots in the family album. Mom and Dad. Two kids in matching dresses. A dog—usually spotted. Standing awkwardly in an anonymous suburban driveway in the middle of somewhere. Squinting into the sun, while Grandpa fiddled with his lens cap, documenting all the moves with endless photos of shiny, new license plates on dusty, sensible cars.

New trees. Saplings, really. Ritually planted by folks who would never stay rooted long enough to see them grow.

Jeanne, in my first-grade class, who had lived there, in that one place, "her whole life!" The cul-de-sac, full of tricycles and snowball fights. And the tiger leaping silently from roof to roof, heading for our house.

But no one would listen.

Women Gathered

Women, gathered for healing.
Most on the way to older. Some faster.
Encouragement. Dream work. Art. Friendships.
Writing. Conflict. Meditation. Theatre.
Fear. Stories. Food. Mostly fabulous.
Don't ask about the smoothies!
Water dance. Heaven. Really!
And then, on the last night, Dance. Patchwork music.
Mermaid hostess, hand extended, inviting each in turn to magic.
Me. Last.
Terror… surprisingly released.
Something Latin beating inside me.
Barely remembered twirling, spinning.
Held, utterly without containment.
Of course, the music ended.
Flushed. Panting. Amazed.
Then the mermaid whispered in my ear, and I was free.

Many Things Are True

Many Things Are True … I am still coughing. This is true.
It's also true that I have, in the past, broken ribs coughing.
Coughing hurts. Then and now.
It's a gorgeous day. This is true.
At least here, where I am. Linens airing in the sun and breeze.
My kids are coming.
Politics are everywhere. This is true.
A Greek word, that.
Something close to "of the people"!
Plural people.
It's also true that politics are hard.
I want to hate the haters. This is true.
It's also true that I try hard not to hate.
Hating does no good.
I have a favorite. This is true.
The one voice I would dare to trust with my girls' future.
And so I speak, tears in my eyes. This is also true.
The water I am drinking is clean. This is true.
I can afford clean water. Many people can't.
This is also true.
I voted. This is true.
Nobody questioned my right.
Many people will have a different experience.
This is also true.

America is hard. Many things are true.
They don't always get along so well. This is also true.
Language creates reality. This is actually true.
Though, admittedly, hard to wrap your head around.
Which language will we choose?
Which truths?
There are bees buzzing among the tiny leaves on the grapevines.
This is true.
A big dog snores gently at my feet. This is also true.
Baby quilts are calling my name. Two of them, needing to be
finished. This is also true.
I am still coughing.Coughing hurts.
Then and now.
Many things are true. They don't always get along so well.
I'm OK with that.
Complexity is what there is. This is true.
Trying to hate it away will never work.
You may say that I'm a dreamer. This is true.
A dreamer dreaming still. This is also true.

In Order to Learn

In my first life, I was a nurse.
Young. Naive. Scared. Juggling.
A small child.
Too many things missed.
Med floors first. A couple of them.
Then surgery.
Before "Grey's Anatomy."
Docs all men.
Nurses all women.
Stress.
Guys on the roof with Igloo coolers.
Babies. More urgent than my own.
Fatigue.
Frustration.
"You don't get paid to think."
Yet, how could I not?
Utterly interchangeable.
Four moments in two years.
I made a difference.
Grief.
The guy with the double knee replacement.
The one whose face I never saw.
Babies. Lost.
My son's new words.
Still young.
Still naive.
Searching for more.

I went on to other lives.
School. Lots. And lots.
Ministry. Thinking often not so popular there, either.
Yet, how could I not?
Therapy. A bit of woo-woo. A magic wand.
Still longing to make a difference.
Not interchangeable.
Me!
Less young.
Less naïve.
A granddaughter.
Then two.
Grey hair.
Insight.
Making a difference.
Mattering for a moment. Huge.
The old desire.
Even stronger.
To be me.
To matter.
A whole new life.
Grandmother.
Each day a new chance.
Hopeful.
Grateful.
Each moment led me here.
A radical shift in perception.
And I am changed.

Leslie I. Bolin

Leslie I. Bolin is a marketing, graphic design, and multimedia professional by day, and after hours, writes poetry, weaves textiles, and designs historical costumes. She enjoys viewing the world through her polarized light microscope and week-long loaded bicycle tours on Tomatillo Absinthe, her trusty two-wheeled steed. Visit Leslie at www.studiosouthpaw.com.

Hover

The Moon
and Mars
unhooked
unhinged
the pull
untried
and still
impinged
Like kites
resist
the wind
at first
then dip
and soar
but
fixed to earth
The spine
the spar
the line
the skin
defying
gravity
to spin
Their
catch and sway
depends
on strands
imbued
and held
with
skillful hands

Music

Before I set bow to cello,
strings vibrating, limbs humming,
coaxing a concerto
of warm sprightly themes,
extended dark movements,
and expressive fuoco phrases
drenching the air with tonal colors,
I must learn the notes
for how you sound
at rest
under the pavilion of our
nocturnal words.
Skillful maestro,
mark the music and
give me the program notes—
your feelings, your sensitivities,
your failures, your regrets
what scares you, what you adore;
give me a sense of your history
so I understand the context
of the composition.
I wait,
my fingers poised over the strings.

Wanted

I want to crack my hard exterior,
this pointless exoskeleton
hungrily forced open,
unafraid of delicate new skin,
outer framework shed,
exposing my tender inside.

I want to escape the feeling
that I am trapped in a snow globe
being violently shaken
by a child interested only in
watching the sparkling swirling flakes
while I stay glued to the base, immobile.

I want my self-worth to hold my hair
while I vomit from temporary binges
of self-loathing,
when the worth I know I have
decides to play a game
of hide and seek.

I want to walk with souls abundant,
who remain unshaken when I embrace my power,
and won't try to tone it down
or steal it from me,
and grin knowingly
when they see their own reflected.

I want your authenticity
to dance a pas de deux with mine
its simple virtuosity
pure and valid,
unfurled and exposed,
embracing its sublime glory.

Bobbing

Halfway below ground
and halfway above,
amid microscopes, mending, and music,
I stare at the glow of this screen.
A miniature, dragon-suited Jimmy Page
holding his double-neck SG,
cigarette perched on his lip ledge,
leans back and busts into his Stairway to Heaven solo.
The screen isn't talking.
Neither are my fingers.
My muse is silent.
I light my hookah.
Exhaling voluminous Skittle-flavored clouds,
blaming the overhead light
for my parched imagination,
I switch on the desk lamp.
In the half-dark
I lock eyes with a stuffed puffin
and my mind wanders
to the deck of a boat in the north sea
where three friends and I
popped the cork on a cabernet
and drank a toast to mark the moment
when we were grateful to share
the sighting of scores of puffins
bobbing about in the troughs and crests
while a sea-sick young man
retched into a trash can.
One of the collective nouns
for a group of puffins is an "indecision."
I smirk at the similarity.

Solvitur Ambulando

Facing the labyrinth
this cool morning,
I focus on the center,
set my intention
and begin walking,
each deliberate step a conversation.

Omniscient Hawk circles near the divine
where I, on foot, cannot
(not for my lack of wanting),
and cries twice.
"Look. Look."
Taking stock of the landscape before acting,
the hawk will stoop when the time is right.
I feel the current of where I'm being drawn.
I see from a different perspective.

I walk on.
Blue Jay settles on a basswood branch, fluttering;
his raucous mischief creating a deflection
among heart-shaped leaves.
The impudent trickster claps before taking flight.
Blue on azure.
Clarity of soul.
Truth of heart.

I tread the serpentine switchbacks
barefoot on stones as warm as fire glow.
Reaching the heart,
swaddled within scents of soil and sedge,
I hold a smooth stone and shell in open palms
and meditate here
where time is elastic.

Ready,
I rise and begin moving.
This circuitous route
has no intersections; paths never cross.
The course is clear
until a single oak leaf falls,
edges dry but alive,
a harbinger of scarcity.
The strong silently let go
to survive harsh conditions.
Abscission.

I walk on.
Grasshopper abruptly alights,
grounded in the power of the pause;
then zips away
undaunted by large leaps.
I attune to my own stirrings.

Winding, I reach the end
in thankfulness
for time given
and lessons learned,
patience in coming and going.
Circle in heaven
and on earth
Complete.
Unbroken.
Turning to face the heart,
palms together,
I bow in gratitude
and once more seal my intention:
Be love.

Doug Bowie

Doug Bowie is always writing, occasionally committing his words to paper. He has perfected the art of "Zen mandala mowing," a creative methodology in which full chapters, pages of prose, are born as the lawn is groomed, and are subsequently lost as soon as the mower is parked. He has, over time, and with the aid of an extensive collection of self-help books, made peace with this. This cutting-edge art form was cultivated in his native state of Maine, and he continues to write, both in mind's eye and on paper, from his hilltop island home in Western Puerto Rico.

When not gathering papaya and avocado, or shooing lizards, he can be found adding to his Facebook page The Sherpa Writes, on Tumblr at How I Left the Mainland and Rediscovered Myself, or at www.ascribeinparadise.wix.com. His preferred topic is the observance of the human condition and all its crazy wonder.

He is also the gracious co-host of Inn Paradise, for those interested in a Puerto Rican retreat from the real world.

He work has appeared in *Seacoast Living* magazine, an entity he was past editor of, and he is currently working on two new books. Follow him on Twitter, @BowieDoug; Instagram, dougb1; livingwiththewindblog.tumblr.com, or Facebook, www.facebook.com/doug.bowie.7.

Midnight Diversions of the Online Mind

Midnight conversations with voiceless kindred souls
benignly begin with mindful intentions that detour.

Like well-oiled trains on tracks of melting butter,
skittering along their way to becoming mindless ramble
and ample distraction.

Our cockeyed locutions playfully crash through
the underbrush of consciousness,
with weary conductors nervously and wildly laughing.

Masking heavy-hearted pathos,
the heaviest of sadnesses haphazardly stacked,
like carelessly doomed games of Jenga.

Fears that wrap themselves in a wooly overcoat of pervasive
double entendres of dark humor.

With buttonholes and long-worn unmended patches, letting the
slightest of light through, eventually drawing the tired-but-genuine
smiles out ... only ... hopefully ... to be followed by the peaceful
sighs that might welcome sleep.

This is the stuff that draws us to log on, to search, this late night
electronic warmth sitting across our laps as we bare our souls and
tap out our literary blood
as we roam ... seeking connection from other heart-weary and
sleep-addled souls ....

The Quiet Aftermath

Sunday silence abounds in the forenoon
while remnants of late-night revelry remain in quiet contradiction.
Full-moon spiritedness and animation
begets an almost eerie quiet on the morn after.

Quietly awakening while the rest of the house still slumbers,
Stealth-like maneuvers try to maintain
the pristine bubble of my gifted sanctuary.

My eyes scan over the black, steaming brew
with hopes it will raise tired eyelids
and gaze with partial wonder at the curious mix
of the sacred and bacchanal still abiding.

Gone are the scrubbed floors and clean tables of yesterday,
replaced now with scattered rubble.
Like an abandoned archaeologist's dig, bits of detritus linger behind
after all activity has long been forsaken.

Late night conversations still linger in the air.
Stories told and laughter born
hang loosely from the lampshades and rafters.
They lie in repose across haphazard ashtrays
and curl around empty glasses and the occasional bottle.
A single unmatched shoe left as a reminder
that exhausted bodies retired casually,
without care or great thought.

Somewhere in the house others took refuge,
and upon midday light will show themselves
as they return in haggard form.

Clean up can wait.
My silent cocoon will soon give way
to the stirring sounds of logy bodies, shaking off their spent shells ...
but for now, it's just me and my pen.

Lost Years

I watched you grow up from afar,
obliged to relive my mistakes every night
as eyes grew heavy, but the mind stayed
alert and unyielding, force feeding the slide show
past my mind's eye.

Clenched lids hopelessly vulnerable
to every missed opportunity, every lost day.
Scraped knees, bruised hearts, tears of confusion,
mourning of pain, yours and mine.

An unending guilt, one you can't release or relieve,
nor should you; it was never expected
and certainly not earned.
The ease of the early years somehow disappeared
like fog on an early morning, lonesome highway.
The sun rises, dissipates, leaving only wisps,
as likely and true as the distance that now separates us.
Words never come below the surface,
content to ride the complaisance of the current atop.

Civil in all its lovely falsehood,
the politeness masking the depth of our awkward quagmire.

Unable to lift the heavy weight of so many lost years,
of so many things left unsaid, never wanting to be brought up.

I taught you to ride the bike, took the training wheels off,
and now I'm left to watch you ride off alone,
deep into the horizon, never looking back ... and it's my fault.

I never put that mirror on the bars,
afraid to have you look backward and see my mistraced steps ....

Failed Free Falls

The heart aches and the mind breaks,
while the soul quakes deep in its boots.
Fear shakes my root chakra alight with "not right."
Or right?
Who really knows what is right or not.

When there is no sense of right and no saving grace,
when that free fall goes from inevitable to reality,
we were so busy trying to make it all perfect
that I forgot to pack my chute.

All the times we fought over pillows
till somehow I just gave up—
ironic in hindsight.
I didn't even bring one to soften my landing.
Heaven forbid I should try to break my fall.

I just need something soft to lay my head on,
to rest and renew.
I should have thought of it all,
since I've now lost my way
from my place on your breast,
where it all seemed too safe, and yet somehow just right,
while I laid my head.

(Paper) Elephants in The Room

And when it was all done,
nothing was left but the tearless crying,

Barren sadness and hollow "victories"
of muck-driven battles over aged appliances and cheap paintings,

Abandoned memories now tainted with ragged edges
and blood stains of sharp-tongued words of exaggeration,

Years lost and uncertain futures now cemented
with the aid of briefcase carriers who know us by the name of "client."

The angst-ridden trail that separated us
somehow conjointly led us to the awkward
inevitability of sharing the same elevator to our demise.

Seated in this room of heavy dullness and worn wood,

just me and you, the necessary officiants,

and the endless paper elephants we pass between us,
signing blindly where oddly bright-colored tags and arrows
order us to ....

Robin Futrell

Robin Futrell is a U.S. Army Veteran, with 15 years of service. She lives and writes in Killeen, Texas with her husband and Benzo the Yorkie. Contact Robin at olitzjam@gmail.com.

Sun Tunnel Kids

Kids in a sun tunnel hiding,
Wondering if they should fight.
Not sure for what or against whom.
The Big Bad Wolf,
The Wicked Witch of the West,
Their demons or someone else's,
Or all the rest of the stuff
From which the world needs saving.

Enough

He touches her with tenderness,
Yet she never feels it.
It's never enough.
While he sees only her,
She believes she'll never be enough.
He tells her he loves her,
But for her,
It's not nearly enough.
She has his heart.
Will she ever believe it?
Will his enough ever be
Enough for her?

Journey

Grounded,
Out,
Wings clipped.
Rest,
Look up at the sky.
Don't wonder why it happened.
Stand up.
Get in the game.
Broken wings
Mended.
Remember, this is a journey.
Be on your way.

Might

Head above, just above water.
Heart shattered.
Body Battered.
Soul tattered.
Things don't matter.
Might not make it.
Might not make it.
But woke up,
Yes, woke up.
Why fake it?
Can make it.
Head above water.
Heart regulated.
Body healed.
Soul better.
Can make it.
Why fake it?
Things matter.
Might make it.
Just might make it.

Unsteady

Bridges, ledges, cliffs, ridges,
Tightropes, balance beams.
No traction.
Fractured.
Without firm footing,
No solid ground.
Slipping, sliding.
Falling—hard.
No padding.
Cramped fingers, tired feet.
Barely holding on—
Always that feeling of unsteady.

Gary Gregory

Gary Gregory is a writer, business owner, and commercial real estate broker. He is a contributing member of the international online weekly, Poem Kubili. Gary currently has three books in progress and posts new stories and poems daily to his writer page; an amazing effort, with four sons, a special needs daughter and a dog running through his kitchen.

You can visit him at www.facebook.com/garygregorywrites

Birth of the New Romantics

Standing on the stage for the first time
together in an empty theater
wondering what this would become
the musicians size each other up
everyone stands for a minute
in awkward silence

The drummer shakes his long hair
staring suspiciously at the guitarist's suit
the lead singer fumbles with her gypsy dress
the choir looks around, fidgeting
the keyboard player adjusts his fedora
the bass player twists her keys
touches earrings beneath her short hair
the horns tune and empty spit valves
dripping pools on the wood stage

There is no leader
no written lines
only one word thundering from a speaker
like the voice of God
in thirty-second intervals, "Play!.....Play!.....Play!"
on the fourth "Play" the drummer tips the high hat
strikes a two-four rifle shot heartbeat
everyone turns to stare
the bass thumps a cautious syncopated line
lead guitar nods out a riff
everyone feels inspiration
hearts synch with the rhythm section
two....four.....two....four
the lead singer drops a descending scale
then rises in intervals to a wail of new words
the choir spontaneously strikes a minor chord
guitar shreds the pentatonic scale
pounding the stomp boxes with his feet
the horn line explodes
blasting a wall of sound
so fierce the singers cup their hands
to their ears to hear their own voices
the drummer silences them all with a cymbal crash
at phrase end

a ripple of cymbal cues the string bridge
swelling, building, pulling the center of each heart
to a fortissimo crescendo of emotion
of wonder at a song never heard before
pulsing hearts, throbbing necks
welling tears in singers
to abrupt crashing end
the lead holds the last word
until her body shakes for breath
and stops
a measure of rest
as ringing echo dies
we look around,
laughing

Taos Song

Your silent words carry me
To innocence
Flying past scarred years
Through pine
To the edge of memory
To dirt roads and hope
And brightness of youth.

Your voice, imagined, unheard
Waiting for mountains
And the ring of the Shaman's flute
Against stone
Above the Magic Circle.

Summer snow sweeps thundering
Mixed with rain between peaks.
The stream swells gently
Stirring early summer edge grass
As red willow stirs blood.

Sun below cloud
A meditation of pure stream
And moving leaf shadow
Cascading through closed eyes
Into my spirit
Bringing The God of Peace with it.

Last sun falls away
Mountain cold descends
The cooking fire cool now,
Kiva and piñon stirred
To warm sleeping child faces.

I step into night
Watch smoke prayers rising
Past Venus chased by Jupiter
And the waning moon
Sliding into the western void.

The first hour of the new day
I hear your voice.
Untouched, pure, young,
Flowing until dawn
Snow melt bringing me to life
At the edge of the parched mesa.

Funhouse

Man, thinking of his own consciousness
Is lost forever in an infinity of mirrors
Bumping into his own image at every turn
Knowing truth waits beside some mercurial veil
Seeking the way out
Startled by clowns
and air blasts
and tilted rooms
or spiral barrels

He stares ahead and walks, or runs
His reflected physique aging at every confusion
Screaming WHO AM I
Hearing the returned voices
This is You
This is You
You are Nothing
You are Everything
This is the Way

But the voices are only voices of other seekers
Echoing through the funhouse
Though Psyche is the goddess of us all
We must tear our gaze away from our self
Stop our ears to absurd shouts of the lost
Look down
The wise know the path out
is the filthy floor

Peace of Mind

Up a staircase from Cherry Street
Is the Peace of Mind Bookstore
Standing there for the first time
Among the cacophonous confusion.

Anything one could believe
Can be bought here
God and gods and goddesses
Books and herbs and talismans
Spells and Scriptures
Side by side on shelves

The Sumerian magi
Was teaching a class
He stopped, welcomed me
Approached me with star charts
Universal mandala of sacred geometry
His small class forgotten
As we discussed the Mystery,
Babylon to Plato and Plutarch.
To sum the millennia of seekers
In the end, I say, is simple.

What is simple is true.
Only this,
Love. Be it. Do it. Seek it.

He agreed in hushed tones
The customers could not hear.
I paid for Thoreau
And read him in Chimera

Deep Pocket

Reaching into my pocket
I draw the contents
To the table.
I spread everything
With a brush of my hand
A divination of bones.
Among the wads
Of hundred dollar bills
Gourmand lunch receipts
A heavy key
Sprinkles of dirt
Lint
Tobacco seed
Toll taxes
Scribbled bits of words
Squinting to a blur
I find
A Pocketful
Of pain
Of beauty
Of love.

Patricia M. King

Patricia M. King is a Maryland based Supply Chain professional, yogi and writer. She has a Bachelor of Fine Arts degree from New York University's Tisch School of the Arts. This is her first publication. She enjoys long walks on the beach, kitten snuggles, sunsets and beauty of all kind. She is grateful for this opportunity to share her words. Follow her on Instagram: @patriciathepoet.

Into the Everything

I like to think
That when we die
Our souls are released
Into the everything

I sometimes imagine the moment
The release and spreading
The feeling of being everywhere and nowhere
And then slowly dissolving into the universe

No longer will I be
Any recognizable form
And yet I will be infinite

Reclamation

An old shed sits
Unopened for years until
The vines weave their way
Around. Green covering the
Old wooden walls and doors
Encapsulating it wholly

And so my feet, they too
Carry me forward towards
The only thing I've known
To be worth the weathering
And that's how I showed
Up on your doorstep
Nature reclaims us all

Mermaid

Did I lose my voice when I lost you
Did you take it with you in a shell around your neck
Is this loss dark magic or something I can recover
Were you just a villain when I thought you were a lover

How am I still underneath your spell
Your words still hanging here make this air so hard to breathe
The waves of grief wash over me and take me in their current
I'm sinking with the dreams you vowed would be until they weren't

Who am I without a pair of legs
Nothing to stand upon
No way to get where I must go
I'm reaching grasping shaking like I've lost my sense of self
Just who gave you the right to take so much from off my shelf

Why did I stake all my dreams on you
I dove right in head first
No second thoughts no looking back
Why did I give you everything before I knew we'd make it
How rash of me to lose it all
How bold of you to take it

What about the kiss to make me whole
I waited for the moment but the moment never happened
It might have been true love but now there is no happy ending
You're gone now and it's over
There's no use to my pretending

Can I exist without this destiny
My substance
It is waning
I'm reducing down to bubbles
And if I never find myself I know just what I'll be
Wholly I'll dissolve
A patch of foam atop the sea

And So We Weep

Man has potential for great acts
Be they kind or terrible
Awesome or awful
Every day we know not
What others will choose
And so we weep

Seeds of our hatred are planted
Often thriving through seasons
Festering for generations who
Have never known the rain to
Give life or the sun to show beauty
And so we weep

While we scramble to erect
Every line of defense
We cast about for answers
That live far deeper than the now
Then comes the anger and disagreements
About the whys and the hows
And so we weep

We weep from those places, deep in our hearts
That all feel the same, they have always been
We weep for each other and for ourselves
We weep with understanding
We weep knowing too well how we
Will continue to hurt one another
And the anger feels incurable and
We are only human
And so we weep

But man has potential for greatness
Not always realized, perhaps one day
It will be used to cure us of hatred
To find love and healing in the darkest of places
For we are resilient, as we have always been
We can believe in the future
While we mourn the now
And so we weep

When I Was Young

I did a lot of stupid things
When I was young, when I was young
I did a lot of stupid things
Because I felt invincible

And life seemed more exciting then
Before this fear of pain, regret
So rousing and inspiring then
When dreams felt close at hand

How wonderful to be so blind
The easy life, when I was young
Hope was my constant state of mind
And my heart wore no scars

How quick it all can turn about
The lessons learned, the pages turned
How painful when I figured out
That I was only human

I dreamed a lot of foolish things
One year ago, a life ago
I did so many foolish things
Because they felt like living

But consequences did unfold
They always do, they always do
The stories could not be untold
And older I've become

But what I wouldn't give for just
A glimpse of me, the me I was
I miss the hope, I miss the trust
From back when I was young

Joseph Kittilson

Where I've been is not as important as where I am headed.
— Joseph Kittilson

Learn the rules like a pro so you can break them like an artist.
—Pablo Picasso

Growing up in the magical forests of Northwest Montana, my curiosity for all things unknown provided a playground of never-ending exploration. At five years old, I recall the old man across the road saying, "Hey, Joey, tell me more about that Monkey Bus of yours." Flying through canyons and floating rivers were what separated reality from the land of make believe.

While there are no certificates and diplomas decorating the walls, I have spent a lifetime seeing all that can be seen. This insatiable craving took me out over the high seas as a sailor. A rough and rowdy one at that, I learned to drink and cuss with zeal enough to kill most, yet survived to tell the tales. A jack of many trades and master of few, exploration has always taken precedence. Although I married and kept a home, raised three wonderful children who have contributed to the delinquency of grandparenthood, my heart has continued to follow paths far into the world, always seeking. My rough, callous hands craft imagination through art with Mother Nature as my teacher, expressing her beauty in woodcarving—not for profit, but for love.

Having collected a lifetime of adventures, I try to share these experiences through the stories I tell. Follow me for a brief moment and enjoy the ride.

The Lamp

If all we ever knew were the good things, we'd never appreciate them. Shaded from the realities hidden beneath what we know are dark truths. Is it bad to know that in life there is also death? We fear the bad things that bring us sadness and pain, concentrating our minds on the good things that bring us happiness and joy.

So you found Aladdin's Lamp, did ya? Well, what are you waiting for? You know the trick. Rub on the side of the lamp like you're trying to clean the dirt from it. It happens every time. The thing starts to rumble in your hands, giving you the scare of your life. In a panic, you let go and watch the lamp soar into the air, spinning in a gentle arc. It rolls over like an Olympic skier launching off the jump, twisting into a double backflip and a barrel roll before plowing into the ground with a thud that produces a plume of smoke that continues to grow and grow. Slowly it takes the shape of a giant man with a long beard, wearing that funny maroon flat top hat with the tassel draped over the side. Long robes of silk or satin fabric flow in the breeze, gradually materializing into human form complete with sandaled feet.

He is elated to be free from the prison that has held him for a thousand years. You are so excited you don't even think to ask him where his food and water came from all that time, or how he kept the place clean inside that lamp. All you know is this Genie is about to change your life.

You dance first on the left foot, then the right, jumping with joyous anticipation. You wait for him to explain that, since you freed him, you are now entitled to three wishes. That's right! Three whole wishes. Great Balls! Imagine what a fellow could do, having three wishes granted by a newly released Genie—a Genie you set free from a thousand years of imprisonment.

Did you pause in your elation long enough to ask this mystical fellow why he was imprisoned inside that lamp or by whom? Are you simply all too ready to dispense with the formalities and get on with this wish granting business? How much money should you ask for? Yes, there must be treasures upon treasures to bask in and jewels aplenty to adorn yourself. Why would anyone need more?

One wish would have done the trick, but now that you're the richest person alive with the wealth to have anything you could possibly imagine, one thing you can't buy is living forever. Yes, that's it! Eternal life with all the wealth imaginable, forever and ever and ever.

Who can decide right away on that third wish? What's the rush? That Genie isn't going anywhere until you get your third and final wish granted, so sit back by your new pile of treasure and have a drink. You have enough money to pay for anything. Servants! Yes, hire servants to wait on you hand and foot. Oh, life is good. Life is better than you've ever imagined it could be. Just think! You get to do this forever!

Remember back when you were poor? When you looked at wealthy people in the world and thought how magnificent it must be? You felt a pang of resentment, didn't you? How they had all the power and money, didn't have to do anything, and could buy their way to happiness, people groveling at their feet for table scraps? You knew you could never be like them, barking orders at someone else, demanding things of them that would bring tears to your eyes.

You saw the corruption brought on by power and how other people suffered. How the wealthy, powerful guy treated them any way he wanted because no one else had cash enough to get by alone. They had to suck it up and take the abuse. You realize all the money and all the power has turned you into the person you despised the most.

You remember the innocent little children, laughing and playing. You remember loving families joining together in harmony, doing for each other the things needed to fill the gaps of necessity. They were helping someone else and just didn't have time to care for themselves. The love shared by families in communal service to one another was joyous and rewarding even when each day was a struggle.

Looking up at the rich guy on the mountain, you yearned to have some of his treasure. Now you have it. All of it. You found your Genie in the lamp, and you are free from your past life of scratching and clawing for enough to feed your family, to take a little vacation once in awhile. Now that you own all of the luxury vacation places that can be had, where would you go to get away? The world in the palm of your hand becomes small and lonely when all you have is all there is.

You begin to yearn for the old ways with the folks down below. They were honest and real, for the most part. This is when you remember how happy you already were when you were working and earning every bit of table scrap you could lay your hands on. A sense of pride and joy came from knowing you gave a piece of yourself before receiving your fair share. You remember that third wish? The one you've been saving? That very special wish? Your Genie awaits.

Patiently he waits, knowing once you have seen both sides—knowing you are pure at heart—you would be willing to sacrifice all you have just to go back. A wicked evil heart would stay and become more wicked and evil, but not you. You want the love and company of the community left behind. You want all of it back so badly you are now willing to ask for your third wish, which comes at a tremendous cost. You now know nothing good in this life is free. The best things come with the greatest sacrifice. Knowing If you are to go back to your old self, you must volunteer to serve your time inside the lamp.

When you are released from your prison, you will know how to live free.

Prom Queen

I'd never felt like this before, nor do I expect it to ever feel like this again. Inexperienced hearts of youth beat harder than any other time in life.

I was barely seventeen when the band played the slow song. We were told we had to stay arm's length from each other. We had spent all day long in preparation for this moment, hanging streamers and lights across the expanse of space only hours ago a gymnasium, now dark and oh so romantic. I breathed in the strawberry scent of her golden hair as we began to glide in a slow circle, rocking back and forth to Rod Stewart's Tonight's the Night. That's right. Everything's gonna be alright.

She wore the prettiest light green dress I'd ever seen. Sleek and smooth, it clung to her body like a second skin. I closed my eyes and held her as close as we dared, yearning to embrace but knowing someone, a chaperone, would step into the crowded dance floor and give us a warning glare.

My fingers teased the ruffled frills of her dress as I gently caressed her shoulder. I snuck a glance into her dreamy eyes, and for an instant, our eyes locked together. My heart raced. Oh, she was so pretty. So soft and so gentle. Her eyes darted toward the chaperone, and when the timing was perfect, she pulled me tight to her chest and tucked her face into my neck. Only for a brief moment lest we get caught.

She whispered something; I knew not what, but I felt her hot breath on my skin and the flames burning my soul. Through the dark chamber of the gymnasium, I heard Rod Stewart singing, "nothin' gonna' stop us now."

This time she pulled me closer, the contours of her breasts pressing into my chest as her lips kissed the side of my neck. My rubbery knees nearly buckled beneath me as I savored the moment ... the moment I had the privilege of dancing with my own Prom Queen.

My Zebco

The rain had subsided, and the sun was warming freshly dampened earth. Oh, how I love the musty smell from my Mother Earth. The meadow between our old dirt driveway and town was coming alive.

One bright morning I was carrying my stringer of freshly caught Brookies and my trusty Zebco Spincaster. I was nine years old at the time. Dad had just walked away after failing to change my mind about a couple of choices I had made. The first one was to cast my line over a steel cable stretched out into the lake for reasons unknown to me. I already knew I could reach out with the tip of my rod and crank my lure over it. The second argument he lost was in my choice of lures.

"Use this Wooley Bugger. Rainbows won't hit that rusty Daredevil. You'll just wear out your casting arm and still be hungry later."

I stuck to my argument that it was easier to cast, and I liked the red and white color. Well, he was right about the Daredevil being rusty, so I dug the spray can of WD-40 out of the dented, old tackle box. I hosed down my chosen lure and wiped off a bit of that harmless rust. Dad walked off defeated, shaking his head, mumbling, "the kid's gotta' learn somehow."

It took me a couple of tries to zip that baby out where I wanted it, but the payoff was well worth my painstaking efforts. I felt the Zzzzzzzzzzzz-plip and watched my Daredevil disappear into the greenish water. Then things got real in a big hurry.

As soon as I gave a little crank on my reel, the line yanked tighter than I had ever felt it before. It almost ripped the pole out of my surprised hand. Whatever had chomped that rusty daredevil was big and strong, and I definitely had a fight on my hands. I don't know who screamed louder, Dad or me.

"I GOT ONE!"

"YOU GOT ONE!"

I pulled away defensively as Dad reached for my pole, not about to give up my prize. What I had was a Northern Pike— a powerful, fighting Northern. It didn't take me long to realize that the steel cable was going to pose a unique problem. In a flash, I grabbed the line with one hand, tossed my Zebco on the rocks, and splashed right into the water for some hand-to-hand combat.

The horror in Dad's voice came too late. I plunged my hand into the churning water, grabbed that Northern by the gills, and jubilantly hoisted my trophy up over my head. For a short while, I was amazed at how much that fish was bleeding until I realized my fingers stung. The blood was mine.

A long story short, the Northern Pike won that fight and kept my Daredevil lure. Although having never had it, I was sentimental about having held a Northern Pike in my hand if only for a moment. I still have my old Zebco, scars on my fingers, and a new … Wooley Bugger.

Batter Up

Stepping up, digging traction cleats into the dirt. Feet planted.

A couple of roundhouse practice swings, tap the edge of the plate with the tip of the bat.

So intent.

Confidence soaring like never before.

A shiny hard hat complete with ear guards.

And a slugger. Yep, the real deal.

Made of genuine hand-turned maple, complete with trademark.

"Keep that trademark up," the coach yelled out from the dugout. "Keep yer eye on the ball."

Heart thump-thump-thumping, knowing Dad is in the bleachers watching.

"That's my kid," he'd say to the guy next to him who was pointing out to left field. "That's mine out there," the reply.

A handful of soft, dry dirt and a good grip on the handle. "Choke up on it some," a call from the dugout. "Elbow up," he reminded me.

The glare from that pitcher kid was pretty mean.

He really thinks he can get one past me.

He glanced over his left shoulder at Billy Bowen, leading off of first base, ready to bolt down the chalk line. Then a quick look to the right at Charlie Nelson, set on skidding into home plate.

Then right into my eyes. He winds up.

Right down the pike.

I saw a flash of white and a pop.

It didn't look quite right to me, so I let it by.

"SteeeeRike!" Called the Ump.

"What? Are you blind?" Called my coach.

"That was in the dirt bouncing on the ground." He always gave me the benefit of the doubt.

"Pick your ball, Joey! Pick your ball."

Ready for the next pitch, I lifted my bat high, just like coach taught me.

The next pitch was so far to the outside; I took a step over the plate just to taunt him. No swing this time.

"Ball one."

This was the one! I could feel it. I saw that piece of leather flying right over the fence long before it left the pitcher's chalky hand.

Here it comes.

I lifted my shoulder and gave it everything I had.

Swoosh! I could feel it connect hard. The ball went sailing up into the sky, and I bolted for first base.

Fast as I could run. Scrambling for traction, I saw my base coach waving me off.

What?

"Foul ball," rang in my ears as I slowed my sprint and came to a disappointed halt.

It went down the third base line and hit the ground just outside the line.

Back to the plate I go.

"Shake it off!" from the dugout. "Next one's yours!"

I could even hear my dad's voice in all that noise!

I fixed my gaze on the back wall and readied myself for the next pitch. I can't miss this one, I thought. My dad will be so disappointed if I strike out. If I could only tap it out into the open inner field and make it to first base.

The next pitch must have been a fastball because I didn't even see it coming. The sickening pop when it hit the catcher's mitt sunk my heart down to my toes.

Oh, the shame I felt. Until the Ump called, "Ball two."

Elated, I jumped up into the air in jubilance. For one split moment I felt as though I had failed, but now I was getting another chance.

My teeth gritted in grim determination; I took my stance. The world completely vanished around me. No sound came to my ears. My vision tunneled to nothing but that menacing-looking pitcher. "Gimme your best pitch and watch it disappear!"

The windup and release sent my target hurtling towards me in a flash. I swung my slugger with a force like never before. The next moment was merely a blur in my mind as the bat tumbled to the ground and my ears filled with the screaming of the crowd. My hands stung like they'd been hit by a yellow jacket. It only took a moment to realize I had been hit by the ball.

The tears rolled down my face—not because of the pain, but because I made it to first base.

Widow Maker

OK, to make a long story short, I just got wheeled out of the ER, lucky to be alive.

I actually died, but was able to swing a deal with Saint Peter by signing away the exclusive rights to the footage of my misadventure.

I had one of those heart attacks known as the widow maker. I was stone cold dead, but lucky for me, I was already handcuffed to the hospital bed after multiple, non-life-threatening contusions and muscular distortions caused by the most ferocious fight I've ever lost. He, Saint Peter, was laughing so hard that I thought I was going straight to the fire—pitchfork in hand— for certain.

The party was in full swing when that big oaf Sergeant Muldoony...... Mul-----Dooooooney. What the hell kind of name is Mul—Dooooney. Showed up with his big, badass billy club and started waving it around in my face, pissing me off. Now I'm not a bad guy, but keep your dirty meat hooks off of my half-gallon jug of whiskey.

I was holding my own pretty well when that 400-pound cop got in a lucky punch and clocked me one in the left cheek. Just before the lights went dim, I saw the flash of pretty chrome jail cell keys hanging on his belt, and my escape plan started taking shape.

Next thing I know, is, I'm waking up on the floor of a jail cell still wet from some other drunk's piss and vomit, and that Muldooney guy was laughing at me. I spied those shiny keys for a split moment, and like a panther in the dark, I made my move. I was full up off the floor, flying like an eagle towards my prize when Mul-Flippin-Dooney conked me on top of my head like he was packing a sledgehammer. He was cackling like an old hag when he slammed the jail cell door behind him. The last mistake he made was to pop a smart-assed remark to me once he was all safe behind those iron jail door bars. "You must have some sort of a death wish, little man."

Holy shit that pissed me off! I've never been more mad at someone in my whole life, but it gave me a crack at getting close to those jail door keys. I retorted through a bloody lip, "As a matter of fact, Copper, I do! I do have a death wish. I want to die of a heart attack while putting it to your sweet, little sister."

I figured he'd spin on his heel and come back inside the jail cell to pummel the crap out of me, and I'd lift the keys on my way down.

No! That isn't what he did. Not at all. He just kept right on walking away. Laughing.

He's obviously too dumb to be insulted.

Time in that jail cell stood still for what felt like an eternity. There were no windows at all, so I didn't have a clue if it was daytime or night-time. I thought I was losing my mind when I heard the most beautiful sound. It was the sweet, sweet sound of a woman softly humming. Oh, it was like honey in my ears and flowers in my soul. Then, I heard the rattling of keys way down the dark shaft of a hallway. Her voice got louder and brighter right up until my eyes feasted upon the gigan-tuous hulk of a woman shuffling towards me out of the dark. She had this vanity thing tucked under a linebacker-sized arm as she grinned at me.

I can't begin to describe the lump in my throat as she set up that van-ity right outside my jail door and began to paint herself all up with lipstick and mascara. She sort of reminded me of Jabba the Hut until she stood up and shimmied out of that cop uniform and bullet proof vest, revealing a bright, red nightie.

I just about shriveled up dry as a desert when she rattled the jail keys in the lock and said, "Hello, sweet cheeks. My name is Daisy Mul-dooney. My brother says you're a real sweet guy. I'm going to love you forever and ever."

I'm not sure what all happened next, but I do remember the pain. A lot of pain. She was squealing maniacally as I faded in and out of reality for a while until I woke up, all busted up and handcuffed to a hospital bed. There was a real cute nurse fussing over me, checking over the tubes and wires sticking out of me. Then, I noticed bouquets of flowers. Hundreds of flowers!

The nurse told me my wife sent them.

"WIFE!" I screamed, "I don't have a wife!"

When I realized the bouquets were all made with daisies, the widow maker hit me.

Tree Langdon

Tree Langdon is a Vancouver writer and artist. Her short stories, poetry and sketches are inspired by her life experiences and by the beauty of the West Coast. She studied creative writing in college and has recently "Written herself Alive" with the Rebelle Society. When she's not writing, she's most likely playing her ukulele. She currently lives with her husband and a herd of roaming deer on Vancouver Island. Tree often spends her days thinking about how to be a better human being and how to leave the world a better place. You can find her at www.EnticetheWrite.com or on Twitter: @treemillie.

tb © 2016

Waiting for Magic

they say crows
remember your face
and watch as
you gather shiny things
trinkets and stones
glass and beads
to embellish their nests
like the colorful hangings in a sanctuary
of a girl
who waits for magic
to whisk her away to lands unknown
and shower her with trinkets
and stones
and like a crow
she remembers your face

Fly With Me

I dreamed I was flying,
each breath released a gentle sigh
as gossamer wings lifted
in surrender to the summer breeze.

I blink and hold a brush,
a long, black wand,
the tip as soft as your eyelashes.

My arm breathes color
as an image drifts into the space.
A shape rises to the surface
through the fog and mist.

You appear in sacred form
and say
fly with me.

Lost

My mind drifts.
Thoughts disperse in tiny cuts
as the whip licks its lips.
Memories break away
in large grey chunks of ice
and crash into the sea
sinking out of sight.

I lose the marks and blazes on the path
and mourn their loss.
I wonder why I throw my tears
against the wailing wall.
Demons drink their tea
while curling in my ears.
They leave a swirling trail
of leaves in the bottom of my cup.
I cannot read them.

Cement is setting
on the furling sails of my ship.
I trace the patterns of the grains in hardened sand
until it falls between my fingers.
As I lose the trail again,
I do not know what course to set.
I am adrift.

You take my hand
and walk beside me as we track a memory past.
We wade through thoughts
that pull us off the path.
I stumble, and you tighten your grip.
When we reach the clearing
where the sun
paints mottled patterns on the grass,
We pause
and then we walk
together into the bliss.

Release

I must release
The thoughts that swarm
In tiny threads
Inside my mind
A swirling cloud
Of calling crows
They spiral down
Into the depths
Of foggy muck
I cannot breathe

I suffocate
And cannot call
My voice is locked
Within a vice
A cage of wire
Entwines my throat
To stop the words
From getting out

I must remake
This life I live
I follow threads
From woven nests
I hear beliefs
Persuade and tell
They call like crows
And draw me in
Their rigid thoughts
I take as mine
My echoed calls
Reflect them back

I am not them

I write my truth
The threads unwind
The spirals twist
To clear my mind
Where secret fears
Are held inside
A wire cage

I raise my arms
Unbind my wrists
And take the pen
To find release
I bleed them out
Unleash my thoughts
I speak my truth
In single drops

Forgive

I carried
packages of hate.
White hot bundles.
Anger tightly wrapped
with many lengths of twisted twine.
I held this burden close
unwrapped it often
and examined every reason.
I remembered well.
Justify.

I held each piece of blackened stone and sharpened glass.
Turned them over, one by one,
and deftly honed their edges.
I invoked a recollection,
the close intense examination
that reveals the pain.
Savour.

I recalled the wrongs
and sliced open half-healed wounds.
I swam deeply in the seething pool
and swallowed daily doses
of reminders and remembering
choking on the bitterness.
My inoculation,
a ward against hope,
on guard against love.
It shut me down.
Lock.

I dreamed a revelation, of wasted years obsessing,
crippled by the sour bile of my choosing.
A change from righteous fever
of angry justification.
It brought imagination, a new consideration,
another way to be.
Reveal.

I walked my weary bundles down a different path.
I held the wounded parts of me with gentle hands,
gasping at the tender touch I had withheld.
I sipped a soothing liquid
that quenched the blackened vessel of my heart.
Summoning the light, I breathed intention.
I held it in my mouth as a treasure,
a small smooth stone that was a word.
Forgive.

Victorea Luminary

Victorea Luminary is a Western Shaman, Animal Whisperer, Writer, and Activist with an irreverent sense of humor. She is working on her first book "Reclaiming My Power — Healing the Wounds of Trauma (Childhood, Ancestral and Past-Life Trauma)." She has spent her life reclaiming her passion, creativity, 'joie de la vie' and helps others do the same. Known by her friends as, 'Big Cow Momma,' she grew up on a small upstate New York dairy farm, and now raises Texas Longhorn cattle. She works with clients, both animal and human, to help them achieve health, balance and harmony.

Website: www.VictoreaLuminary.com
Facebook Pages: www.facebook.com/SoulfulRelationships
                      www.facebook.com/VictoreaLuminaryWriter/
Twitter: @VictoreLuminary
Instagram: @victorealuminary/
Pinterest: www.pinterest.com/victorealuminar/

I Weep

I weep for the mother who learns that her only child has been killed by terrorist's bullets. I watch as she grasps her belly, where her child grew years before. The gut retching pain so potent it knocks her to her knees.

I weep for the father who disowned his gay son, who just weeks ago was killed in the attack in Orlando. I watch as the father sobs and a flood of tears cascade down the glass and over the frame of his son's 6th-grade photo.

I weep for the sisters and brothers longing to say how much they loved them, how much they miss them. I hear them now screaming the "I love you" that was never before said aloud because they were rivals who fought tooth and nail while growing up.

I weep, for the emotionally and physically exhausted who live in war-torn countries as they wait in inexorably long food ration lines, dodging bullets as they head home empty handed.

I weep for the friends far and wide who feel excruciating helplessness.

I weep for those wondering when, not if, the next attack with come.

I weep for us, the witnesses, the watchers, the record keepers.

I weep for humanity, the animals and all sentient beings.

I weep for Mother Earth.

I weep…

In Which Pocket Shall I Carry You?

There are several pockets I could choose...
The back pocket of my ripped and faded jeans
would allow you to see where we've been.
In the front pocket, you would be bounced about
with the small change and lint that lies within.
Neither of those will do!
Certainly not! Not for you.
I know what I'll do!
I shall tuck you into the pocket of my comfy denim shirt
Remember the one, the one I stole from you
It's the color of your eyes
It's strong, yet soft and very wise
Like us, it's been around for years.
Over the years, its sleeves have dried both happy and sad tears
It's been here and there and seen it all
It has hung on fence posts and pegs on walls
It's been wrinkled by your hugs so strong
In that shirt I know it is to you that I belong
So, yes, yes, yes!
That's what will do!!
It's just perfect, perfect for you!
Adventures ahead and sweet memories behind
We never know what we will find
Next to the heart that loves you best
Snuggled in safely, inside that pocket on my chest.

Truth of You

Shed every ounce of your humanness, every label and belief.

Stand before me courageously naked.

Invite me into the sacredness of your inner sanctum and allow me to caress your gleaming spirit. I deeply inhale your sensuously sweet scent and savor your effervescent soul until I am drunk in love. I am hopelessly enthralled, ecstatically drowning in the exquisite truth of you.

Final Goodbye

It was a Thursday evening in late May when he said, "Victorea, I am going to see my parents soon."

Always trying to lighten a heavy subject, I quipped in my best Brooklyn accent, "Have you seen them yet? We won't worry until you see them."

I knew full well what he was trying to tell me. My Rock of Gibraltar was preparing to leave me. I put on my stoic cloak choking back the tears hoping he didn't hear my heart shatter.

He was just shy his 104th birthday and had lived a fairly happy life. He had accomplished what he loved best, building and farming.

I wasn't ready to lose him, yet I would never ask someone to stay who was ready to go to the great beyond.

I remember when I was very young, maybe 5 or 6 and him warning me, "I am not going to be here forever, I am going to die someday, and you're going to need to take care of yourself."

I would cry, "No, Daddy, I pray I die before you, I never want to lose you!"

That night I asked him the usual questions, "Do you want to go the hospital, or see a doctor?" "Are you in pain?" "What can I do for you?"

"No, I don't want any doctor, and no hospital!" He said sternly. "I just want to die peacefully at home in my own bed."

He had granted me so many wishes in my life, that I was honored to grant him this, his last wish.

For six days I sat by his bedside. He was apparently comfortable as he never moaned or cried out in pain. He would talk with me and then turn to talk with the 'others', those who I knew had prede-ceased him. It seemed clear to me that he was having a pre-death life review. I had only heard about life reviews after one leaves their physical body, this was the first surprise as I played the role of stew-ard for his transition.

I learned so much in those six days. I learned that we can leave this earth plane consciously, that we can choose when we leave and how. That we do not have to be sick with a terribly painful disease to leave our body, that we can simply decide it's time to go.

Secondly, I learned that those who are dying may enjoy physical touch. Early on I sat with my hands in my lap at the side of his bed, sometimes talking, sometimes quite. Finally he surprised me and said, "Victorea, please hold my hand." It hadn't dawned on me that touch would be something he would like, that it might be grounding for him, connecting him to the earth plane while he was investigating the other realms.

With that simple request, he taught me a very valuable skill and when his younger sister, my Aunt Mary, was in hospice for five short days, I was able to comfortably hold her hands, stroke her forehead and massage her arms. I wasn't afraid to disturb her because my father had taught me that those who are dying may actually enjoy being touched.

On Monday night he asked for a beer. Seriously? My father? That came clear out of left field! He wasn't a drinking man, but if my dying father wanted a beer, so be it. I ran down to the corner store and picked up a six pack of Heineken. I opened one bottle and used a teaspoon to place a few drops on his tongue.

"Blech!" He shouted. "This damned Fitzgerald's beer will kill 'ya!"

Oh my gosh! I hadn't known where he was in his life review, but I now realized that he was back in the 1930's. How fun was that? My father was somewhere back in the 30's in a bar ordering a beer. Wow.

That was the good news; the sad news was I knew it wouldn't be much longer before he would be gone.

That night when I left, I said, "I'll see you tomorrow, Daddy, I love you." Choking back more tears.

"I love you, okay…tomorrow." He said as his voice faded off.

The next morning, I arrived around 6 a.m. and sure enough he was there, waiting for me.

"Maybe we could call the Priest maybe that would help him to go." Aunt Mary said.

By now, five days into her beloved brother's death process she was frazzled. She couldn't take much more of what she was interpreting as his suffering. Yet, I did not sense on any level that he was suffering at all. I think it was her fear of death, more so than what he was actually experiencing, that bothered her.

In that moment, I realized what I had said to him the night before and why he hadn't gone yet. The night before when I said, "I'll see you tomorrow." He promised to see me, and as always he had kept his promise.

Aunt Mary was the religious one, my dad not so much, but I called the priest who administered Last Rites around 10:30 a.m.

My father was asleep, or appeared to be, the entire time. Shortly after the Priest left, my father's eyes opened, and he asked me to clean him and change the bedding which I was more than happy to do.

Later that day, he remained pretty quiet. Every so often his eyes would open, and he would look at the wall at the end of his bed as though he were seeing someone there. I have no idea who, as I never really have had the gift of sight.

That night before I left about 8:30 p.m., I began to cry. I thought he was asleep and I began to whimper a little. He turned to me and asked me, "What's wrong?"

I knew that tonight I had to say good-bye for the last time. So, I told him, "Nothing is wrong, Daddy, nothing is wrong. I love you. You take care of yourself okay?"

"I love you, too." He said.

Then it happened, I saw for the first time ever! Next to me on the side of his bed close to his head appeared a strong stout older woman dressed in a button down house dress with an apron. As soon as I finished saying what I said, she crossed her arms and I could hear her saying, "That's my boy; I'll take over from here."

Was she really his mother, my grandmother? She had died eight years before I was born, so I had never met her, but she looked just like her picture. She was about five feet tall, stocky, and strong. From the picture I could never felt her energy, but let me tell you, this woman standing next to me was a powerhouse! Now I knew where our family feistiness came from!

I went home for about an hour and when I returned both my father and Aunt Mary were resting peacefully, she on the sofa and he in his bed.

Back home in my own bed, as I shut my eyes, I saw the house they were in filled with beings of light. All the prayers I and others had said and all the angels and Archangels I called in were in that house. It was absolutely full; there wasn't room for a toothpick!

That was the night my sweet father passed peacefully in his sleep. I believe it was in my saying, "I love you, take care..." rather than, "I'll see you tomorrow..." was what he needed to let go.

These are some of the most intimate moments I ever shared with my sweet Dad. The beer, the "I love you's" the tender touch of his hand. He was and still is the most important man in my life. That is not to say that the men who I have loved have not been important, they have, but in a different way. The way I see it, when a man is an exceptional father, provider, protector, and teaches his daughter through example, acts of kindness, understanding and compassion, he sets a very high standard for any man she chooses to share her life with.

My father was a great man, and I am truly blessed. He was the first man who ever fell in love with me and loved me just as I am, warts and all. He was also my first true love.

I have heard it said, and I believe it's true, that no matter what happens between them the love between father and daughter is unbreakable, infinite and everlasting.

My father and I had lots of disagreements, but in those six short days everything was forgiven. When someone dies, they cross through a veil, but are never far away. The challenges of this lifetime fade, and only love remains.

To All Children

God bless ALL the children of the world.

This child is my child. This child represents all of us, regardless of race, religion or belief system. He is your child. He is everyone's child.

What these children living in war-torn countries have endured, have seen and experienced at this young age should NEVER happen to ANY child. EVER!

How can a child who has endured war, violence, abuse and loss of family and country ever hope to live a 'normal' life? Trauma remains deep within the psyche and the cellular memory. We know this from the research. He and those like him will be scarred for life.

War creates more war—because it creates people who disassociate, who cannot feel, who shield themselves from their feelings and from being vulnerable and open. They are the walking wounded. They physical wounds may heal, but the emotional wounds last a lifetime and are passed down through the generations.

Trauma victims learn to cope and survive rather than live and thrive.

We are killing off our species. Sure more will be born, but they will carry the wounds, the emotional wounds of trauma. Those wounds will be inherited by future generations. Is this what we want for our children and grand-children? NO! Why would we want this for the children of another country?

May the child that still lives within us, that innocent little being we were when we were young reach out to the heart of this child and all like him.

There is a part of us who knew then and still knows but is afraid to share the wisdom - how to love openly and honestly. We have repressed that knowing because we too were hurt and traumatized in our own childhoods. May that gentle, loving child within each of us reach out to those who are still children, who are not yet adults, who are vulnerable.

May love pour from our hearts to theirs, across borders, across time and space. Sending a soothing salve of love, a LOVE BALM to their little hearts.

May the inner child of all those who promote war for their own personal gain – those who are making millions off war - may their inner child wake up and realize what they are doing to humanity to future generations. May their inner child be HEALED and put a stop to the wars they have created.

Let's WAGE PEACE not war.

I pray for all beings, for all the innocents worldwide.

I pray for each of us.

I pray PEACE.

I pray LOVE.

I pray HEALING.

I pray ENLIGHTENMENT.

I pray AWARENESS.

I pray PEACE within the HEARTS and MINDS of ALL HUMANITY.

WE MUST PUT A STOP TO WARS. Our world depends on it; our species depends on it!

Amen.

Sarah Martin

Sarah Martin resides in beautiful South Florida. She is a poet-
ess, inspirational writer, and speaker on mindful, compassion-
ate living. For her, words give color to this beautiful, wild life and
she loves sharing her fiercely honest insights with the world. Her
writing isn't pretty — it's raw, messy, and authentic. Sarah speaks
and writes from the soul, pieces reflecting all the various seasons
of our lives. She also teaches therapeutic movement classes and
mindfulness workshops, helping individuals harness their dormant
desires. She believes we all have fire burning inside of us, waiting
for a window to open, for breath to give birth to desire. When she's
not teaching, Sarah enjoys leading her Into the Wild retreats, travel-
ing the world, hiking, relaxing with her cats, and creating stories
to touch upon this human experience. She enjoys sharing her daily
inspirations for living the best life possible and wants to impact as
many lives as possible while she's here. Please follow her for more
inspiration: FB: www.facebook.com/sarahspeaks3113/, Instagram:
Sarahspeaks3113, Twitter: @SarahSpeaks3113, Blog: medium.com/@
sarahspeaks3113

Softly

Go softly, he whispered,
for I am made of water
and broken yesterdays.

Go easy, he cried,
for my path's been paved with lies
and many foolish tries.

Go fast, he urged,
for I want to miss the ache
that will come with losing you.

Go slowly, he nudged,
for I'd be a fool
to give away even a moment with you.

Go gracefully, he murmured,
so I can tell my heart
the nights holding you were true.

Leave marks across my skin,
he begged,
so I remember where my soul has been.

Give Me Your Wild

I ache for someone who,
Rather than stain my cheek with tears,
Paints another smile line on my eyes.
I choose someone who,
Rather than saunter around tenderness
Longingly gazes towards the deep end of the ocean.
I want someone who,
Rather than ravage me and leave when the clock strikes dark,
Wakes me in the morning with a look that quells my deepest fear.
I desire someone who,
Rather than encourage my demons to rise from deep slumbering
Shines light beams onto wounds, whispers healing balms to my
soul.
I need someone who,
Rather than shake from my thundering intensity
Leans into my storms and dances in my rain.
I crave someone who,
Rather than pretend not to be wild
Howls at the moon, his darkness reconciled with his light.
I demand a wild man with messy hair, sultry voice, eyes filled with
wonder and lust for life, a laugh that carries profound appreciation
for this crazy life.
I don't want a man.
I want a warrior.

Collision Course

I turn the last page of the chapter entitled "Tumultuous Love Stories" and sit. I allow it to permeate my very existence, to seep into my Being. All the amputations, those pieces of my heart, begin to ascend into the graveyard where broken hearts eventually graduate to once their masters have relinquished the residual grief and angst. They are met with other broken hearts that have come before and are guided to a place of eternal rest, where their cracks and fissures may be mended in time and sent out to Earth again whole and to a new sender, one who has not yet been jaded from the dusty desert of unrequited love. Goodbye, heartache drenched in disappointment, your invite into my life and heart is cordially rescinded.

As I turn this page into a new chapter, one yet unwritten, with no middle or end, I pause. I pause not to dwell on what was, or give any more of my precious energy to what will never be, but to say thank you to what has come before, for preparing me for this very moment. I pause to relish in the knowing that I am ready to be met with a love so great my Earth will shake again when our eyes meet, my feet will fail to hold me up, and my lips will fail to hold back what they yearn to say.

In this next chapter, there are more rainbows than shadows, more windows than closed doors, more honey than vinegar, and more laughter than tears. There may even be a white picket fence, equipped with rocking chairs on a wide-open porch, green pasture for miles, and birdsong to lull us from sleep to the next sunrise. I'm ready for you, Great Love, one that trumps all other loves, and all the hopes and dreams met with fulfillment that dance in your light.

Then there are those whom you see coming from eons away: those soul mates you dream of and name your unborn children after before you've even set eyes on one another, the one you dance with on foreign lands and distant oceans. The ones arriving quietly, who, if you're not paying attention, you could easily miss them, except they recognize you too.

And then, your eyes meet on this Earth plane, and it's a subtle shift, undetectable by all but the most acute eyes and ears. No, wait, it's not the eyes and ears; it's the heart that delivers the confirmation. It's the imperceptible yet minutely detectable tiny crack in your armor; it's the thud of the weight you've carried for so long, falling to the ground. You look, expecting to see an evil being; instead, you see fear embodied as darkness. But when he comes into focus, the darkness is transformed into light with his touch. All the parts of you hurt by love, left abandoned in the throes of passion are loved back to life. He leaves soul tracks on your body. No wound left unhealed. His kisses erase the marks left by men who didn't know how to love you.

It's combustion. It's collision. It's a soul-on-fire kind of feeling; impossible to ignore. It's a change in course. In one moment you've resumed the eternal dance again, the one your hearts have etched onto your souls. He takes hold of your soul and vows to never let you go again.

"Where have you been? I've been looking for you," he says. "I've been in you all along. Some people needed to crack me wide open before I got to you, so when I saw you again, my heart would know what it was like to be held." My heart has been yours for all time, you reply, with the softness of love you didn't know you still embodied. You know you've spent lifetimes loving this man. You sink into his arms, knowing eternity is your birthright and love your purpose.

Illuminate

As the waves roll across my body,
Mother Nature embraces me.
I lick my lips and taste the ocean's curiosity.
The sheer magnitude of all I am and all you are
Becomes clear in the droplets melting on my bare skin.
Suddenly, I know I am the Universe.
I am YOU and YOU are me
And WE ARE ONE ~
Separateness is an illusion.
Shh, don't say it too loud.
Those with power in their throats and blood on their hands
Might collapse from the knowledge.
Their weak infrastructure may crumble
The light piercing through, cutting untruth,
Glass shattering and voices rising.
Which side are you on?
It's a paradigm shift, ya'll.
Our weapons are truth
And love.
Theirs: corruption and greed.
The truth shall set you free.
Wake up, illuminate.

Morphine

That fire
On your tongue
Hit my lung
Collapsed
Punctured
Poison seeping
Oozing, weeping
Veins constricted
Morphine-addicted
Ensnared breath, vacant eyes
Fix me, deliver me the drug of my demise
Feed me 'til I satiate
Then leave me to emaciate

Jackie McCullough

My most cherished and honoured role is being mama of four amazing human beings who are the loves of my life. I am a school teacher who loves to inspire my class to be their best selves. I love music, singing with my daughter in the car, mountain biking in the mountains with my grandson, flyfishing with my boys, and enjoying nature around me with my furry companion Maple. Being a lover of mountain life, nothing is better than waking to the smell of fresh pine on crisp mornings, spending endless days in the mountains, road tripping, campfire watching, and hanging around the kitchen in our home with my family, while laughing about...I don't even know what! Writing poetry has become a new exciting adventure for me that I hope to continue on my life journey.

© 2016 JM

#1

She surrendered to the tranquility of the sun,
the beckoning of the moon,
and the steadiness of the sky,
calling her gently, guiding her back
to a forgotten place,
reminding her of where she first became.

Unable to unstuck, she searched
and resisted the irresistible,
no longer able to hold the wild within.
Her will was far stronger than the pain,
more fierce than that which held her back.

Will found the vulnerability she couldn't hide,
and broke free, forcing light into the darkness of her being.
It burst open the walls bolted and chained by fear,
sealed with blame and guilt,
freeing her from contracts promised.
Replacing blame with acceptance,
guilt with compassion,
and fear with the freedom of love.

Knowing and accepting,
believing and becoming—
she won.

#2

Sunset settling in for its daily rest,
she takes a deep breath, soothing restlessness,
calming her with its subtle reminder to embrace peace,
trusting her heart could endure the demons which took hold.

Gusty nights held a steady embrace,
carrying the deep-rooted loss far into the clouds,
with twists and turns and twists and turns along the way,
whisking them away until remnants were beginning to be forgotten.

Lightness attempts to ease in, replacing the shackles it once owned,
promising to release the forgotten one hidden within,
offering permission to become the beautiful she never knew.

Uncertainties restrain her, at first unwilling to surrender,
but an unrecognizable whisper inside repeated with an energy she
never knew—
just jump, my love.

#3

A cool breeze wallows through the window at dawn,
rising carefully and aware.
I will you there in unconscious slumber.
Semi-awake, foggy and soft,
you consented to be with me.

Sensing you.
Feeling you.
Wanting you.

I create your every move.
Holding me close,
nuzzling in,
keeping me warm.

Your scent permeates my senses.
You let me taste your lips,
soft and supple,
safe and protective,
reminding me of what I love.

You give me just enough
to keep me where I stay,
longing and unable to be free.
It was all I needed for that moment
to sustain and replace the sadness
of your leaving.

#4

I'm reminded of the beauty of you.
Waking from slow slumber, rising to nature's melody,
rain trickling, singing the sad song it knows only too well,
reminiscent of days spent lazy and easy.
So perfectly intertwined,
fiercely colliding, unleashing untamed passion,
engulfed in a world only we knew and understood.

#5

Unraveled and on edge,
peeling layers of self-doubt and regret,
overwhelming thoughts unleashed,
clouding the images of what they were.

Imperfections glowing neon,
reminding her of all she was not,
dwelling there,
stuck,
unable to release.

Stricken by the failure of her authentic self
and fear of standing alone,
she waits for reprieve,
searching,
unable to find.

Time has seemingly stolen her youth
with ingrained, unrealized wants,
panic of years gone by,
with few to repair.

Dreams fading before her eyes,
unsure of new beginnings,
static and motionless.
She screams to be heard,
to be unleashed and freed,
learning all she had to do first
was love herself.

Janice Raquela Mendonca

Around two years back, Janice Raquela Mendonca, also known as j.r.m., found the one thing that set her heart on fire, burning with a passion only recognizable to those who follow theirs. She embraced the chaotic madness of words. She has found that writing somehow always brings therapeutic healing at the same time it drains her of the emotions that would threaten to drag her down.

Janice is an undergraduate, currently in her second year of degree college in the city of dreams—Mumbai (India). This 28-year-old writer has battled the life-threatening, rare illness known as Wilson's Disease. Now that she's stable, she's currently working on a book, recounting in detail the experiences she has undergone.

You can find her on Twitter @JaniceRMendonca
on Tumblr - jrm-poetofficklehearts
and on Facebook www.facebook.com/Writerjrm/
or, you can personally contact her at
janiceraquelamendonca@gmail.com

© 2017 j.r.m

Reasoning about hope...

Hope is the flickering flame that burns in the dead of night.
Forever eluding,
mysterious in it's ways.
Hope is that noose around your neck
slowly choking your breath.
Hope is the water filled in your lungs as you drown.
Holding out hope is like writing your suicide letter
explaining things, hoping someone will eventually understand you
after you've gone.
Hope is that hand that reaches out pulling you out from the danger
zone.
Hope can be anything you want it to be,
but only in your mind or heart depending
on which houses hope.
Learning to recognize when a situation can use hope can help make
life much easier.
But foresight is a superpower.
And logic is a luxury not everyone can afford.
We're all just winging it,
hoping hard for hope's sake
that we will be the one saved
that we will be that 1% fraction.
And sometimes hope is just a stranger in a stranger land.
Lost, wondering how it ended up there in the first place.
Hope is the lie you feed yourself every night before you go to bed.
Hope is the pillow upon which your dreams sleep

Image © Marián Uhrín (Czech Republic), used with permission.

Madman in Love

Your head rests upon my heavy heart,
I feel your lightness dissolve my heaviness.
Calming the raging tempest that swallows me whole.

I hear whispers in the corners of darkness
And it is you calling my name out of the wilderness

Stalking shadows follow me everywhere I go
It's you lingering close by,
with watchful eyes.

When the cool wind blows over the nape of my neck
and when a gust of wind ruffles my hair
It's your touch that soothes this burning soul of mine.

Your love has drawn a curtain over my eyes and
I see you,
I feel you
in everything.

When you undress yourself from the cloak of invincibility
I see myself in your naked vulnerability and unabashed honesty,
the one who I'd like to be
against all odds.
for you.
for me
for us.
Standing there, humility is awed by the sight of you.

Without realizing,
without a warning
you have broken down the barriers
that safeguard my heart in a fortress.
You have carved a niche for yourself
leaving your essence
in every corner of my body.

Whatever I do,
however far
I try to escape
from you,
You are
in the wind that blows on my face
when I make a run for it,
You are the dry mud that flies
everywhere my feet touch the ground.
You are in the salt of my tears.
You are every fucking where!
The very air I breathe -poisoned by your laughter.

I hear you whisper loudly in the rustling of the trees as I try to cover
my ears.
I feel you strongly in the swaying of coconut trees in the afternoon
breeze
I feel you in the echo of every strum of my guitar.
I hear you call out my name in the rain storm
I hear your cries in the crashing thunder
I feel your sadness in every dark cloud.
I hear your voice in the chirping of the birds.

You are my heart's compass
Haunting me yet guiding me
my map to all things unknown
my lighthouse on the sea shore.
my anchor in the ocean
my wings in the air.
you are that rock mid ocean
upon which every violent wave
never fails to visit.
you are the dancing northern lights
that decorate my night sky.

Ten feet deep drowning in a pool of frenzy,
I want to sink to the bottom and I want to be saved
in the same breath.
I can't think clearly
my mind is never made up
ever since that one fateful day
You crossed my mind
you haven't left
You have captured my heart,
entranced me in the aura of your love
Everything's forever changed
in a single twist of a whirlwind
I see the world with your eyes,
I love with your heart
I cry with your tears
I feel deeply with your senses.
For you have infected me head to toe
mind body soul, heart spirit.

Darling I am a madman in love.

Her Resilience

Her blood on your hands
blends into your skin and fingernails
dripping from the edges of your fingertips

plip
      plop
plip
      plop.

Striking the washbasin
reverberating
the only thing you hear.
Deafening.

You try to control the flow
in your hands
but the blood still manages to escape
sand slipping out of grasp.

Nothing is in your control
and all is falling apart
like a domino effect.
All you can do is sit back
and watch with your hands tied
the mess you have made.
Now bear the consequences.

Your bathroom sobs
confined to its four walls,
knowing you broke her heart
you wear the stains.

No matter how hard you try
these stains won't wash away
with mere water and soap
or bleach for that matter...
but son, you already knew that, didn't you?

And right now you wish you could
just peel your skin off because
the deep red color of blood
stabs your eyes.
Blinding your vision, your foresight,
distracting your thought process,
you can't think straight.
It haunts your very conscience
has darkened your soul to a shade
unrecognizable.

You hear her cries,
you are tormented by her sorrow
haunted by the sadness in her eyes
intimidated by the conviction in her heart
awed by her strength to keep going despite it all.

Yes I get It now.
it's not the heartbreak that haunts you
But the beauty in her resilience.
It rattles your bones.

Nostalgic Intoxication

…and then the song
came on the radio
and I knew better than
to switch the channel…
I turned up the volume,
till I felt the words swim
underneath my skin,
floating in my mind's space
and gravity isn't the culprit
this time.

I thought…
I was strong enough
to resist the
pull of the past,
the tight grip
it still has over me.
And that wave of
emotion which I have
been running away from,
washes over me,
tainting my eyes,
trickling down my cheeks

Nostalgia you intoxicate me…

It's all too much to take in.
Paralyzed, my heart
is beating but
I can barely feel the 'thuds'
in my rib-cage…
unable to move,
my feet off the breaks.
The engine revvs
—a metaphorical announcement
of the arrival of shooting
indescribable pain
accelerating through
my body.
I'm stuck,
crumbling,

crashing, but fuck!
Every fucking word pierces
through my bones
reminding me of the
beautiful state of pain
you left me in,
I can't help but romanticize
everything you left me with
as you wrenched my beating heart
right out off my chest.

Nostalgic intoxication
I can't help but let you in,
just to feel him running through me
for one last time.
I have traded my peace of mind
for the longing you have carved
in every corner of my body.
Pulling me in,
shutting me out,
shuffling me,
dragging me by my legs
sometimes squeezing out
every last tear drop.
Exhausting my lungs.
I breathe because of the
history between us.

I left pieces of myself
like a breadcrumb trail
for you to find your
way back to me.
And now I am
left with nothing
but a hollow self..
a nameless victim
of nostalgic intoxication.

The words stings me,
cut me,
break me…
bend me
but never heal me
from the heartbreak
you gave me.

The pull,
the sweet intoxicating rhythm
beckons my yearning heart
to bend to the wills
of your torture…
that gentle smile,
those soft eyes,..
that can warm up
the Antarctica…
And shit…I know
better than to
surrender to the
whims and fancies
of your heart's desires.
My heart is foolishly
in love with everything
you do to me.
Be it heartbreak,
suffering,
be it love
or hate…
Nostalgic intoxication
you sly motherfucker
Creeping, crawling, under my skin.
Who is the bigger fool for letting you in?

Woman

There are many layers to me.
like when you a peel a rose petal by petal,
and with every petal plucked
my color becomes
richer
darker
deeper.
I'm rage.
I'm sadness.
I'm the woman reflecting on a sunny afternoon.
I'm moody,
I'm endurance,
I'm strength
I'm a fist clenched tightly.
I'm a taboo
I'm a revolution.
I'm expressive.
I'm a recluse -an island to myself.
I'm self sufficient.
I'm independent—your chains don't shackle me.

My layers will confuse and amaze you.
So don't try to analyze me with your bewildered mind.
I can't be categorized
labeled
or defined.
Words will always fall short of
the power I behold in my fingertips.

I was born to give life.
Born from your ribs.
I was born to give meaning to life.
—to fight to struggle.
—to cry, to laugh, to smile.
I was born to win, to fail.
—to crawl, to climb.
to embrace.
I was born to fall, to fly.
——to rise. to inspire. to encourage.
to share.

I was born to be a
daughter
a sister
a friend
a girlfriend
a wife
a mother
an entrepreneur
a warrior
an aunt
a grandmother
I was born pure and innocent but this world branded me a bitch,
sometimes a witch...
to the evils I became a victim.

I'm the unborn daughter you aborted.
I'm the one you gave up for adoption.
I'm that "One".
Look how I turned out,
Can you recognize me?
I'm the one you lost.....
I'm the privilege you turned a blind eye to.
I'm the essence of every woman.
I'm all the above and much more
your mind can't even begin to process.

You cannot define me.
You cannot contain me—for your shackles don't bind my spirits.
You'll never catch me.
You may have raided my body
but you can't raid my soul.
I'm the wandering heart
I'm the gypsy soul.
I'm earth,
fire,
water,
air.

I'm fierce when I need to be,
I am wild, you can't tame me.
I'm uncontainable.
I hold the oceans in my palms.
I hold the skies in my eyes.
I hold the stars in my smile
I hold storms in my tears.
I'm a force to be reckoned with.
Don't mistake my tears for a weakness
therefore they are my greatest strength.

I'm not your property
I belong to solely myself
I was created out of man,
but, I'm twice the man you'll ever be.

Bill Munley

Computer Systems Consultant, Writer/Poet, Film Photographer.

This is his first published writing work; hopefully, not his last.

Bill grew up in Springfield, NJ. He currently resides in Jenkins Township, PA. Father, widower, wallflower, Reiki Master, medium in training, city boy in a rural setting, and a collector of socks to brighten your day. A quiet, humble, handsome man living life through writing with his heart on his sleeve from his corner of the room.

Life at the speed of WTF

We don't take the time to smell the roses
or listen to a friend pour his or her heart out.
If we slow down, it's "What's taking you so long?"
If we speed up, "You're going too fast."
Fucking confused with life.
Past, present and future.
What's the cure?

Take a breath.
Step off the world.
Be here.
Be now.

Do
Be
Do
Be
Do

I bet you thought that was just a chorus in a song ...
Be you.

Fallen Heroes

The tap of the drum.
The click of their heels,
matching beat for beat
in this your special parade.

Family tears fall as they march by,
carrying you with honor
to your final resting place.

The snap of the flag as they fold it,
the creases tightly made,
layer upon layer,
the final corner tucked in.
A loud click of the heels
as the flag is presented.

Attention!
The team of seven stand tall,
their rifles at the ready.
Aim, Fire.
Aim, Fire.
Aim, Fire.
Order Arms!
Your 21-gun salute shakes the birds from their nests.
They fly overhead in formation as if Mother Nature
is paying her respects.

Taps is the final song
played by a single horn.
Its sound echoes across the valley.
Its message to the world:
A hero has passed,
The world a better place because of him.
Honor him as he honored you with his sacrifice.

May all our fallen heroes rest in peace.

On the Edge of the Forest

Here on the edge of the forest,
where the road ends and the trees begin, there is a sign:
Do Not Enter
Private Property.

The sign is old and rusty,
its edges torn and shredded where the nails were used
to attach it to the tree.

I wonder how long that sign has been there.
I wonder if the owner still cares about the forest.
I wonder why they nailed the sign to the tree instead of on a post.
I wonder what the penalty is for walking in these woods.

I walk around the tree with the sign and into the forest.

Traffic sounds fade behind the trees as I walk into the silence of
man.

I could not help myself. Nature called to me.

The breeze through the tree tops says, "Shhhhh!"

Leaves upon layers of leaves from seasons past rustle under my
boots.

I see no animals, but I can hear them.

The scratching of the squirrels claws as they run up the tree.

The bees buzzing around their nest, and then flying off
to find fresh flowers.

The birds, each species in their own language, sing along, creating a melody. The woodpecker's beat, the blue jay's leading cry, and the robin's backup vocals. It's a strange but happy tune that echoes under the forest canopy.

In the middle of the forest, a small field exists. Empty and alone, it appears to be lifeless. I sit on the edge.

It's cool here. The tree cover blocks the sun on this cloudless day. I stretch my legs to capture the warmth from those happy rays.

Above the field, I can see the hawk floating on invisible updrafts, gazing down at me. I wave a hello.

Peace and quiet surround me. After awhile, my breath and the gentle breeze are in rhythm.
In time, my heart becomes the only sound I hear. The glow of my heart chakra surrounds me. It's as green as the forest, and it expands and contracts with the beating of my heart.
As the sun drops, its shadow slowly closes over the field. When it reaches my feet, it's time to leave. Just enough light to follow the path out.

As I approach the beginning of the path, the sounds of man return. Cars, trucks, and people, all singing their own tune, no melody here. We need to listen to Mother Nature. She knows what she's doing.

We're just babes in the woods.

Still the Grass Gently Weeps

It's 1 AM.
The grass feels cold against my neck
As I lay staring into space.

The quiet, almost deafening, broken only by the cricket's mating
call.
Jealous? Yes, I am.

The sky dark,
A deep black and blue,
Shimmery,
Like the surface of a lake,
Just upside down.

Air—crispy as it breezes by my face—
Keeps me awake for now
As it chills my toes.

The moon,
Half empty yet
Half full,
Glows down on the valley.
Are there others staring there, too?

A single star shines
So bright that the clouds seem to fear it.
They drift around its shine as they float by.

Bat wings flutter.
Moths duck and cover.
I feel the owls stare.
Whoooo

Footsteps,
Soft brush strokes in the grass.
The snort and sniff of the fox,
Unsure what I am or why I'm here.
I don't know either, but we agree
He should go away as he rushes across the field.

Settling back,
What was once a tickle
Now brings an itch.

The sky seems indifferent to my plight.
If I only had wings to take flight,
I wonder what I would look like from up there?
Who tells the story?

It's now 2 AM.
Am I through
What am I supposed to do?

Does the earth feel my weight?
I feel its weight on me.
I hold onto the grass to keep from spinning off.

Do my thoughts weigh me down?
Does the ground push back when I sigh heavily?
Does the spirit in the sky pull my spirits up,
So Mother Earth gets a break from the heaviness I feel?
Are her winds cleaning my soul?

The soul—
A hole,
Not whole—
Whistles a tune of loneliness
As the chilled breeze flows through.

Cold is the heart that beats.
Still the grass gently weeps.

A Walk

The air crisp, the sand cold, the waves whisper
In the morning low tide, hugging the sand
For what little warmth it has left from the day before.

Many think it's a lonely place,
The beach, in the early morning.
But, here, daily, life begins anew.

The night's high tide washes away all signs of yesterday.
Pounding surf, churning seas, white capped waves cleanse the sand.
On occasion, they may leave a shell or two for
the early tourist or jogger,
Maybe some seaweed, too slimy to grasp and pull out to sea.
These tiny remnants the only sign of life as the day begins.

The salty, briny scent of the ocean water
that has soaked into years/layers of sand
fills my dreams so vividly my nose itches.
Seagulls cry as I walk by in the darkness, disturbing their slumber.
Even the sun thinks it too early to be here, hiding just below the horizon
Yet this is my time on the shore alone with my memories.

My feet can't stand the cold any longer.
I walk to the gazebo and sit on the bench, facing the edge of the world.
The black sky slowly changes as the sun wakes from its slumber.
Purple and grey clouds glide across the sky.
Brilliant yellows streak towards me as this massive globe of fire rises.
Orange glows across the waves, shimmering
with the gentle, rolling tides.

It's all a blur as the tears fall.
I feel her hands on my shoulders—
A gentle but firm squeeze.
Is it the ocean breeze or her voice whispering?

I love you, always.

Elle Newlands

Elle Newlands is a hybrid, which makes her complicated but she is okay with that. An actress, photographer, writer, she spends her days juggling characters, words and pictures. Elle's poetry was first published when she was 14 in "O Mice and Men" a Scottish anthology. She has also been published in "Self-Management for Actors" (now in its fifth edition), Showfax: Actors POV, Backstage West and is a regular contributor to Elephant Journal.

Originally from Scotland, she is currently enjoying the sunshine of California, where she hikes with her dog, rides her horse in the mountains and talks to nature.

Instagram: @photopoet_elle
Facebook: www.facebook.com/wordsbyelle

the flight pattern of crows

let your heart be the bird
and drop the stones
that keep you grounded.

let the flight pattern
of crows, be your map to magic;
skipping like stones
over blue pond, with the ripple
of a cloud chased breeze.

look to skies with stars
and promises of freedom
and circle on a solo trip,
while melting into flock.

let your voice be heard,
whisper down old memories
with courage and abandon,
wildness sewn into your heart.

stay awhile, up in heaven's attic
with the nesting doves.
don't look down,
with hands in pockets
filled with clenched fist and regrets,
instead;
let your heart be the bird
and your light
be their thunder

the million year sleep

wrapped in lichen velvet cloak
she sleeps,
Queen of the forest.
set to rest in the nests
of ancestral memories,
she glides from here
to there
and maps her journey forward.
and it takes
more than a minute
to set to rights
the circadian songs of
misunderstanding,
the questions
of her place
in this world,
of where she walks
with light
and what is hers to take.
this road,
this path of honesty
and truth,
lined on all sides
with grace,
she purposefully sleepwalks
into waking and glides
with careful steps
lined with gratitude
and satin thanks.

and it's here
she kneels before herself;
the only one to follow,
the one who has the answers
and she knows this now.

the Scarlet years

I crocheted wings
to my ghosts
and allowed them
to fly on home.
Heavy stitching
holds the past
in weighty embrace,
with memories of lightness
and insouciant relief
from days of denial.

A short flight
from here
to there,
held in place
by concrete butterflies
and the wish of feathers.
Because this
is where
the in-betweeners live;
in flights of fancy
and longings of tomorrow,
sewn into daydreams
and dandelions,
held fast
by heartbeats
etched in stone.

I looked to the heavens
and watched them fly;
stained glass specters
of my youth
and the daughter I was,
translucent and colored
by the Scarlet years
and I wished
upon the stars
of me,
shooting through the dark.

Here,
in this space
of infinite possibility,
my eyes seek out truth
and the nebulous silhouette
of a girl
exploding into night

the abandoning

she let it all go,
took a pair of scissors
and cut out the pain.
with scalpel precision,
she excised
and carved herself into pieces
unsure of what was left.
parts perfectly stacked,
she placed herself in the corner
and stood back.

she had always felt
that her rage
should be neat,
despite it's burning beneath her skin
and making her feverish
but her reflection
told of chaos and mess within
and for this she felt conflicted;
her mirror, had clearly lied.

it was not reflecting
fairly or justly
of the long night's journey
she had walked
many times over,
instead
distorting truth
into side show carnival freaks,
demonized and traumatized
into believing she was broken.

so with words,
she carved into her marrow
to surgically remove
their influence;
lies and violence
each whispering of youth
and times of disempowerment.

so with parts of her on the floor
and stacked neatly in the corner,
she stepped into a new skin
and swept clean the abandoning

100 yard line

and there was a moment
when I was 20,
that I forgot all of my fear
and I kissed you back;
you,
a stranger in the rain,
in the small hours
of a Sunday night in Glasgow.
me,
the girl
whose hand you brushed
opening the same taxi cab door

kismet,
fate,
accidental longing?

you held onto my fingers,
just a beat longer
than the here and now
and a spark of something
passed between us
lingering in the air

you stepped back, I followed
as you stepped again
straight into my field of being
my 100 yard line
and you walked right into me.
a different door opened
and a lasting moment was born
in a kiss; the kiss
that lives on my lips still
with curiosity and questions
and the heat of something illicit,
something wild and crazy
and forever.

and there she stood,
a girl who was kissed, unlocking
a meandering path of abandon
to try on a different skin.
a girl who thinks about you now
and wonders,
were you one of the ones,
or just the one
who swept me off my feet
for 5 minutes in a troubled time
and gave me hope that I was worth it.

in the passing of years
and many kisses later,
the girl considers that night
in the rain, wet to the skin
with a stranger,
who brushed hair from her eyes
who truly saw her
and it was romantic because
there was no end, just a beginning

Joy Wilson Parrish

J oy Wilson Parrish shares roots with Vermont, Texas and Louisiana. Her essays, articles and poems have appeared in journals such as Rebelle Society, The Tattooed Buddha, Coffee and Sweatpants, and The Galway Review. Her second book of poetry, *Rust*, will be published by Wildfire Press in August 2017. She currently resides in Southwest Michigan.

Amazon: author/joywilsonparrish
Twitter: @joyparri
Facebook: www.facebook.com/JWilsonParrish/

© ® Joy Wilson Parrish, 2016

3 Am

The God of Insomnia tucks his rolls into robes of saffron
jumps on the bed with double chins bouncing and calls the exhaust-
ed from their futile prayers:
please please God let me go to sleep.
The Sandman hastily pockets the Eucharist and flees.
Without regal stance or royal wave or quiet courtly call to arms—
the God of Insomnia heaves his portly rump upon the smooth
leather of a Harley Fat Boy
and zooms up and down my bedroom walls,
the loud Vroom Vrooom, the chant of Loud Pipes Save Lives
echoing from his fleshy, smacking lips.
It is my sleep deprived sanity that pleads for salvation.
I have sung him the eulogy 7 times 7 nights into dawn and still his
relentless chafing chases
my dreams and drowns out my Zs.
pleaseGodplease,Ihaveaninterviewin4hours but
Insomniac God apparently has no fucks to give.
I furtively close my eyes.
Fat fingers snapping, sparking at my sheep mid count
sudden explosions of fluffy puffs in midair light up the room!
lightening shards slap against the closed shades of heavy eyelids,
shades that snap up and roll up thwack thwack wakey wakey.
My saving grace, the heavy mug—it too denies my respite,
the taint of his urine floats within my warm milk
he dances the flamenco across my sheets and laughs, the hateful
bastard.
The God of Insomnia has signaled the choir and the coffee pot
begins the morning devotions.

Avalon Pond

Deep wood shade in Sunday morning stillness
the loon's mournful note rent the misty shroud above the water.
Nostrils flared, heady scents of tamarack steeped memory
for careful sipping
the moss and boggy loam green beneath my feet.

Our silence, understood, a comfort wrapped round my shoulders
I sat damp and chilled upon fallen birch, a curl of parchment bark
my wedding ring

Listen: a mystery still splashes a crystalline cadence,
a final mountain snow melt, somewhere, onto rocks.

A fragile pink lady's slipper, a silent dancer within the fiddleheads
Jack from his pulpit led the choir of trillium at your feet.
The orchestra of memory played on with you as conductor
on that morning out of Avalon, when Spring was young
and I forgot to think of death.

A Past Life

I remember where we were
the cool, deep morning fog sliding up against field stone walls,
the hem of a blue mantle damp with dew, that other life a world
away and October—
October waited, pacing restlessly out on the periphery.

I remember the way we were, that stolen moment
the joyous laughter rising, bouncing
bouncing off of birches and aspens and the silent retreat of the lives
we were supposed to be living
and no longer could.
Seed pods pregnant in opulent shades of umber and pearl, bursting
into the wind that
fed the valley, birthing miracles:
your hand brushing mine with a quiet breath of expectation,
the invitation within seraphim eyes.

Love hid on the underside of burnished leaves and behind
russet, ruffled mushroom skirts
peeking shyly out at booted feet dancing,
dancing over pathways that we were never meant to cross.
We glided across each one, hairline cracks forming on the stones
of someone else's foundation.

I remember that autumn life,
the scent of decay within the falling leaves,
the streamers of honeyed sunlight unfolding from canopies of gold
and crimson,
the iridescent drops of morning dew suspended from the brim of
that worn
leather hat, falling in slow motion as I descended
in slow motion, holy
and haunted into the halo of your arms.

My fall from grace.

The darkening was a stealthy beetle, a crepitus within the dried
leaves beneath our feet
the glade a shroud of violet grey and the mellifluous canticle of the

woodland voices stilled.
The lone bell sounded from the steeple on the hill
your death announced by feathers floating to the ground,
this secret swallowed whole to reemerge
choking, upon this page.

Eulogy for a Friend

Rest in peace, my faithful frigidaire from the Sweeney Todd Scratch and Dent Barely Used Appliance Emporium. For 15 additional years you chugged along, suffering through sticky handed toddlers and school aged children swinging from your freezer door. You chilled countless holiday turkeys and beers shared among friends. You valiantly protected my chocolate stash within the confines of a bag of field peas, never betraying the hiding place within your frozen heart. Only four times, perhaps six, was I required to forage for gold coin, to hastily call upon the medics to rescue us both from some malady of yours, real or imagined. I remember that time your water line froze and exploded, the constant stream overflowing the cat box in the basement below, long undiscovered. A subsequent evening stroll to the laundry room was rudely interrupted by wet ankles and the bump of cat turd icebergs against my toes. Such shrieking as tumbled clothes basket chaos ensued.

I grew accustomed to your relentless chugging and snorting, the constant boom chakka lakka whirr wicky cough belch song you belted out throughout the quiet night, taking comfort in the lullaby that told me you were still on the job. I learned to cha cha to that crazy cadence of your over stressed motor, my colicky babies lulled and soothed back to sleep by the fierce vibrations as the too warm dented side was gently pressed against distended tiny tummies. So many good times shared.

And now, as I mop the gag worthy melted chicken and cherry Popsicle life's blood spreading across the kitchen floor, as I toss the fetid remains of $200 worth of newly purchased victuals into the garbage bin, I bid you adieu and say a prayer for peace and prosperity.

...Because you, my friend, are about to cost me a shit ton of jangle in replacement possum patties, tater tots and equipment, not to mention that jacked up delivery charge plus tip, (for hauling your old ass through slender Victorian hallways, around 90 degree hair-pin turns and down two flights of crooked stairs.) Yes, Adios, you mother fucker. I'm going in for the newer model. This time I'm getting the fancy, younger, sleek lined version, the one with a dual ice maker/margarita dispenser and a computer embedded in the door so I can keep up with social media while contemplating my midnight snack choices. I'm getting the fancy digital monster with the Australian male Siri who purrrrs : "hello you sexy bitch, care for a cocktail?", instinctively knowing it is a drink I need not the stumble to the coffee pot. My wine will be a precisely chilled elixir and my Aldi's fish sticks, (bought on sale), will be solidly frozen, not the other way around. My milk will not curdle and my butter will not melt, two weeks from the "sell by" date. My eggs will cease to freeze into solid rubber bullets that fit into child sized hands intent on delivering a deserved comeuppance on unsuspecting bully neighbor kids. Life will be a perfectly chilled, humidity controlled, bowl of cherries.

Just kidding. I'm going back to Scratch and Dent. I need that money for books and ink pens, but thanks ever so much for the memories.

Persona Non Grata

Storm clouds gather, the wind delivers the smell of rain
and—something darker,
the steeple stands tall in shadows of deepest mauve and coal.

Whispers strike with glass and pebbles brought from the gutter
on gusts of laughter
dust devils dance and whirl through legs
tanned by Sunday service stockings,
now crooked seams and laddered holes stand stark
against pale flesh.

Whispers sing…*shoo. shoo*: Brittle dry corpses of unspoken words
and
husks of nightmares rattle, the murmur of wishes dead before the
birthday candles
met the flame.
Shoo shoo.
New growth choked by ancient ivy, tendrils reach for an innocent's
ankle, the hem of her
dress trails into the mud. The bell in the tower begins to toll.
It is Palm Sunday in the village but the crocus never bloomed.

Low voices intone beneath the wind
ebb and carry, flow and ebb
the tables by the rectory wear checkered cloth
in tattered strips and shreds of red
the swing on the playground swings back and forth and
to and fro, to and fro
but no childish laughter fills the air. Where are the children?
Behind that door? *shoo shoo*

The ladies from the rectory march out and move in unity
fat arms laden to feed the holy brethren
Willow baskets without lids over flow with—chicken legs? —and
towering cakes
of pink and cream and loaves of bread, a violent green
Sweet tea jugs, a rosy hue, swollen beetles perched on the rims
matching aprons splashed well with red, shriveled hands hold pans
of battered tin,
Church lady casseroles placed heavily on to trivets made of
graveyard bone. A feast awaits.
Spiders fill the sugar bowls and the dust begins to rise.
shoo! shoo!
A smothered cough and en masse they turn as one.

Black holes are where their eyes should be
shuttered windows to where their souls once housed
Grins stretched tightly against black, broken teeth
dead grandma chests heave against tattered gingham blouses
shoo! shoo! naughty children! shoo!

But where? Where are the other children?
Her hand outstretched, the fingers gone but armed with a hymnal
and Tupperware
a pulsing offering beneath the lid
a bit of gristle, a tuft of hair
shoo! shoo! my child, hissed the bloody lips.
And shoo was right and so shoo I did, running fast enough to out
run the dead,
when I awoke in the morning I was safe in my bed.
my doll safe on the chair, the dog asleep on the floor,
and a small Tupperware container snuggled next to my head.
shoo, shoo.

Whitney Poole

Whitney Poole is a Virginia based writer, though her poetry reflects her own deep Southern roots. She's most known for her poignant wit and a modern style that simultaneously alludes to a forgotten time. Whitney has found her voice in poetry while writing her way through personal transformation, discovering that true beauty lies within the rubble. Her self-appointed task is to show this truth to others. The rest of her time is spent wrangling two beautiful children and contemplating ways to battle her passive-aggressive peach tree.

Instagram: @whitneyleepoole

Cataclysm

Delving into my depths
This path of discovery
Creation
Feels like a war zone
Or an abandoned forest
After the fight is done.
There's rubble
And refuse
And a gray cast
Overlaying the land
A pervasive sense of exhaustion
Leaving no room for hope
Or joy
Or plans beyond the necessities of life.
Until a dream is dreamt
Is it possible to step out of the wasteland
Of destruction?
What jarring event
What cataclysmic occurrence
Will be required
To breathe life
Back into
The half dead?

Locks

How many pieces of myself
Have I barred and barricaded
Hoping to avoid the pain of loss?
The fleeting beauty of love
Not enticement enough
To lure me from my cage
The one built by these hands
Welded with fear
Strengthened by determination
Forged in anger's heat
The key assiduously misplaced.
Leaving me now with a choice:
Cleave open this lock
Or wither in my stubbornness?
Lonely in my solitude,
Brittle in my fortitude,
Or expansive in my courage...

Heart (This is how it's done)

Brave is the heart
used and battered and bruised
dusts itself off
stands up and says
here I am
fill me up
spill me out
whatever you do
just don't leave me dry.

Courageous is the soul
who says it's a good day
for I've been used
I have been loved and feared and hated
I've been abused
I've been held close
I have lived, lived, lived.

Fierce is the battle weary spirit
who does not put down his bow
but instead says I am always here
always ready to stand up
to stand out
to be the shield
to be the support for those who love
for those who live
for souls who yearn
for those who grow.

And fortunate are the ones
who have the battered heart
and the courageous soul
and the battle weary spirit
who stand before us and say
this is how it's done
Who stand there and say
don't give up
look at me
for I am bruised, I am weary
but I am fulfilled
so when you're weak
look to me
I will show you how
I will carry you
I will spur you on
I will cheer for you
I am here
this is how it's done.

My Gift

Gratitude lights a fire in me
Liquidity in my veins
Full of appreciation
For you're a Gift
Such a light in the dark
That distance doesn't dim the glow
My hope:
That you Know,
that you Feel,
What a Gift you are
My bright star
In a sky full of sparkles
But the one to whom
My eye, my heart,
Is continually drawn
There is a force, an energy between us
So strong—
I cannot help but feel the pull
Invisible strings,
Touching, tugging
And when I crawl away to hide
I take these strings
And wrap them around me
Like a hug
Like a comfort
And gratitude seeps from my eyes.

Treasures

I think back and recall so many times you said
I was beautiful or crazy smart or talented
Or So Strong and how proud you were of me.
Always, always, I heard these things as you said them to someone else
Not to me.
I watched you preen, like a hunter who has bagged the finest kill
Or a man on a search for an artifact
Thrilled with the treasure he found for a steal.
I was an acquisition.
Something to pet and call your pretty
Something to elevate your value in the eyes of others
Something
Some Thing.
This is not how one cares for a Treasure.
Treasures should be stroked, loved, adored,
But more often in the silence of communion
Than in the throng of a crowd.
So I am off to be my own treasure.
I am off to celebrate myself
And never will I be a source of ego nutrition again.
No, I will be the fertilizer for a Soul
And the bloom of my own.

Jen Pope

J en Pope is a dreamer, storyteller and poet. Some of her favorite occupations have been as a transitional mentor, yoga teacher, and shamanic practitioner. The multifaceted emergence and process of discovery kindled by shared mentorship through online groups such as Write Yourself Alive, The Writer's Pocket and The Lion's Lair have proved life-changing for her. These forums continue to be catalysts in her journey of evolution and discovery and her growth as a writer. She feels extremely grateful and fortunate to be a part of this diverse community of creators while they are continuing to achieve individual success in more ways than previously imagined possible! She is currently writing a book based on her personal experiences in dreaming things up and watching them manifest. She can be reached at riverpopes@gmail.com, or on Twitter: @riverpopes.

© Jen Pope

Breathing

I spent my time
Caring for the two of you,
My husband Michael
And my sweet brother David,
Fighting the fights of your lives.

I breathed the same air with you,
Which sometimes made me choke.
Did that drowning feeling come
From feeling your discomfort
Or from my own tears
As I tried to hold them back?

At times my breathing in,
My breathing out,
Reminded me of the sea
Where we used to collect agates and seashells
Before we left our coastal home
To search for the doctors in the city.

The steroids made you big and changed your features,
But you were still in there, Michael.
Even when cancer invaded your brain stem
And you could no longer speak,
Our love for each other was constant.

Radiation burned you, brother David,
Inside and out.
You reminded me of a fragile baby bird
Fallen from the nest,
Bones with some skin hanging on,
Wanting so desperately to live.

It was a journey with its gifts, too.
Like the times the three of us found ourselves
Tangled up together in a pile on the floor,
Cushioning each other during a slow fall,
Untangling ourselves in the relief of laughter.
Or those quiet moments of discovery
When we shared slices of eternity.

Three years of moving into changes,
Then suddenly, within three months,
Both of you were gone.
So was I.
Oh, unlike you, my body was still here,
But my heart had closed without me knowing it.
I took a grief bath in tears that refused not to fall.

It's been a couple of years more since then.
I'm still here at your place, little brother,
Where you offered us shelter in the city
And where cancer claimed your body, too,
In a form so different from Michael's.

I am thankful I'm not homeless now,
Like the many who camp all around
This inland island
Of tight-knit houses in the transportation corridor.
It's a place bordered by train tracks on one side,
The freeway on the other,
Under the flight path of the airbase nearby.

No planes, no trains, no freeways—
We had agreed, Michael,
Before we found our little home
Where we planned to retire,
Perched on the edge of paradise.

I remember how we were surprised!
It was part mobile home, part build ons.
We were pleased with all of the windows
Overlooking the river as it flowed both ways.
Sweetwater making its way to the sea.
Tidewaters moving opposite, bringing the salmon.
They would jump into the talons of eagles
Who would fly to their nests high in the trees,
In stands on the mountain across the river.

My words came back through pen scratch on paper.
My visions appeared as I first picked up little kid's water colors.
Before that, my visits with the luxury of paint
Were confined to latex on walls.

I am not the one I was,
But I am steadily becoming.
I have learned the value of surrender,
The quickening as I evolve
Back through the revolving door
Of being more alive than I have ever been before.
As the words flow, they reconfigure me
Into someone else entirely.

Midwife of the Soul

I intend to be a midwife to the soul,
To shine a light at the crossroads
Where possibilities are born
In present moments.

I want to breathe through
The contraction of what is known,
Inviting the expansion of what is not yet defined
But waiting to be discovered.

I invite ceremony
In visions and in quests
Beyond the limitations
Of my current memories.

Help me to listen
Through the beat of my own heart,
To dance to the music of my spirit.

I long to create through
The love and joy of my heart
And live in the flow
Where surrender is victory,
And sorrow is only
The shallows of deeper meanings.

Ravens

I often tell my mom stories that lift her depression and loneliness. They make her laugh until she slips into her fog again. She tells me her 85-year-old body will long outlast her mind, that she feels stuck and no longer wants to live. It is a fate she has been afraid of for many years. She hasn't touched a brush to canvas in a long time, and her paints have dried up in their tubes. She feeds ravens on the deck in front of her house, and they visit her most mornings. They never cease to bring out the childlike wonder in her. This is a story she always experiences as brand new every time I tell it.

She heard the ravens calling
As she rose up from her bed.
She hurried to the kitchen
To gather up some bread.

Ebony feathers
They left upon her deck.
She stuck them in her cape's pocket
As the bread they commenced to peck.

After they had eaten
It was the strangest thing …
They circled in a cawing dance
She found herself center ring.

They cawed to her, and she cawed back,
How she wished that she could follow.
No sooner thought than it was done,
She was flying over the hollow!

To her joy, she'd sprouted wings
And was rising to the sky …
Toward the sea they all did go,
It was wonderful to fly!

From swoop to glide, both high and low,
They coasted and drifted in glory.
She knew that if she ever told
Not a soul would believe her story.

Too soon the sun was setting low.
They escorted her back home.
She smiled while drifting off to sleep.
She thought to write a poem.

While waking up to morning's light
She'd set the teapot steaming.
With a sigh, she peered into her cup.
"Oh, I've just been dreaming."

But as she put her cape back on
She touched a feathery feel.
Her heart suddenly skipped a beat ...
She knew that it was real!

Across the floor, she danced and hopped.
They welcomed her to their pack.
She cawed through her new shining beak
And never did look back!

A Letter to My Muse

Okay, I know you're in there,
Inside my still beating heart.
Thank you for taking my hand,
Guiding it to write words I need to see.
When I get afraid of my dark,
You are intimate with the essence of me.

I love when you stay awhile,
Whispering to me in our moments,
Even taking me over
When I think I won't find you.

You bring me secrets
And a variety of ways to unwrap them.
Sometimes we laugh together,
Cry together,
Discover and dream how to fly together!

It's you I seek while I hide.
You trick me into discovery.
Your cadence fills my senses,
Dances with me as I dream,
Wakes me as words spill through my pen.

You open me when I am closed,
Hold me as words are delivered.
You work in your own version of time;
I am thankful when you step into mine.

Turtle

We were meeting up with relatives camping for winter in the desert. The campers from Washington and Colorado had arrived. Montana folks were delayed due to snow. We were of the California contingent. The eldest of the uncles, Eltjo, would keep the fire burning at the main camp while the rest of us split up on our separate adventures. We agreed to meet back in the circle on certain dates. (Unless, of course, we were delayed due to too much fun!)

Michael and I traveled to the ruins at Casa Grande first. We explored for a bit together and then he wandered over to the museum. I was getting a feel for the place, so I promised to meet him at sunset.

I saw a man in Native American clothing, standing alone. He sang a song in an ancient language I did not know. I was captivated. It was a thing of great beauty. I felt it deeply. Michael came back to find me standing alone, tears still streaming down my face.

We settled into camp for the night. The next morning we got a call on the cellphone. Michael's aunt and uncle were close. We agreed to share a ride with them to the casino for breakfast. We looked at each other and laughed as they drove up in their big old Buick. We climbed into the backseat and soon were riding down the road in what felt like a huge velveteen couch with a car wrapped around it!

Uncle Dwight was buffet hungry, and Aunt Jo could hardly wait to play "Wheel of Fortune." I couldn't care less about casinos. I was interested in listening to Uncle Dwight playing tour guide as he drove, though. I watched as he pointed out creosote bushes alongside the road. He told how one could make a tea with medicinal properties from that plant. I made a face as I remembered my mother-in-law Grace had given me a taste once. It was pretty bitter, but she said it was good for aches and pains.

We were the only ones on the lonely road, so I was surprised when I saw a cardboard sign with a painted turtle and an arrow beneath it. I tried to point it out to Uncle, but he missed it. Soon I saw another sign, bigger than the first, with an arrow pointing to a side road.

"There's another one, turn here!" I exclaimed. So, to humor me, he turned that ship of a car off the main road.

"There's nothing out here," he said. "No houses for a yard sale that I can see. Just scrub."

"Please, let's just go a little further ..." I pleaded.

"Okay." He said. "But it's a good thing I've got gas."

Michael started to laugh, making some crack about his uncle being famous for having gas.

Dwight threatened to roll up the electric windows and lock them from the front seat so that Michael could get the full effect from the back seat.

I saw another turtle sign, another arrow. The road had changed from blacktop to tar and gravel, and we could see up ahead it was getting narrower and was just rutted dirt.

"Sorry, Jenny, there's nothing out here. We'd best turn around."

"Stop here!" I yelled.

He hit the brakes so hard it was a good thing the windows were up! As the cloud of billowing dust dissipated, I motioned to another sign. It pointed to a rocky, dirt trail on the side of the roadway. We could see some Teepees and four wheel drive vehicles parked nearby. It looked to be quite a gathering! I jumped out of the car before Dwight could hit those electric door locks.

"What do you think you're doing?" He said.

"Follow the signs, come back for me later!" I answered with a grin

Aunt Josephine shot a glare at her husband, and then turned to shoot an even more potent glare at mine. "Are you going with her?"

He just smiled and said, "Nope!"

Then she started hollering. "You're not going to let her go hang out with a bunch of hippies and Indians are you?"

"Does your cell phone work out here?" Michael asked.

I showed him my phone still had bars. Jo was still hollering, cussing, too. Dwight was just shaking his head.

"She does what she wants to," Michael said, giving me a sweet wink.

I waved, promising to call back before dark. I took off at a pretty quick clip, just to make sure they didn't try to stop me.

As I reached the end of the trail, I saw a circle of women around the campfire. One looked me straight in the eyes and smiled. "Turtle Woman, we've been waiting for you!" It felt so right to hear her say that. I wasn't even too surprised!

There were, indeed, some Native Americans; as well as an assorted mix of men and women. Most of them had long hair. There were professors and anthropologists too!

I wandered around to various areas where they were teaching and demonstrating different things. I polished myself up a fine piece of abalone for a necklace while they told how the indigenous people traded for articles from far off places. I learned about the benefits of barter while listening to others talk about how to survive in the desert, how to find food and water.

I walked over to an area where people were standing in a half circle, throwing an ax at a wooden pole. I got to do it, too, but it bounced off to the ground.

"Come over here." And this old guy motioned to me.

When I got to his group, he handed me a spear. At least it was lighter than the ax!

"Aim this spear at the middle of the circle over there." He pointed.

I tried, but I've got short arms and not a lot of muscle. Everyone laughed as we all saw I had gotten nowhere near the circle, let alone the center of it! He handed me the spear again.

"Now take a good look at that circle. Close your eyes and see it in your imagination. Keep those eyes closed. Can you see it right there in front of you?" I could imagine I did. I nodded. "When you feel ready and can see it clearly in your mind, muster up all of your intentions and throw, keeping your eyes shut. See it land right there in the middle of that circle."

I threw. People started laughing. For a second, I was afraid to open my eyes. Several people pointed. There was my spear, standing up in the dirt, in the center of the circle!

I had a wonderful day surrounded by interesting people, who had plenty of food and water to share. They were great to hang out with. I had even learned some good stuff! As folks were walking back to their camps, some of them asked if I wanted to stay with them. It was getting close to sunset, so I thanked everyone and said my goodbyes.

The sun was still warm, so I squatted down for a little shade behind some bushes while I dialed Uncle. He hadn't answered yet when I saw a billowing cloud of dust behind his big white car as it barreled down the road. Dwight answered the phone.

"Where the hell are you?" He yelled into the phone as he passed me up. I made my way through the bushes.

"Right behind you!" I laughed.

He hit the brakes and backed up. I got in. Aunt Jo was going on about how everyone in the car except her was totally out of their minds! She described in great detail all of the terrible stuff that could have happened to me!

My Michael gave me a big hug and smiled that smile of his that always touched my heart. He looked into my eyes and said, "Did you have a good time?"

I proceeded to tell them all about it as we traveled from dirt to gravel and back onto the pavement. And Uncle Dwight never ran out of gas.

Cari Greywolf Rowan

Cari Greywolf Rowan, a writer of prose and poetry, pursued a dual major in World Literature and American Studies as an undergrad. Her Master's degree in counseling led her to the mental health and addictions field where she refined her skills as an astute observer of human nature. That career morphed into a holistic approach to healing as a Certified CranioSacral Therapist and led to listening even deeper to her sister and brother humans. With a multitude of poems and short stories and a novella and her memoirs in progress, she howls in the language of human nature, spirit, and the natural world. She has been published in the weekly international online poetry site, Poem Kubili. When not doing creative word dives, she is busy hiking the mountains of Western North Carolina with her camera, enjoying the delights of nature with her partner of 23 years and their Corgi, Marcus. Find her at Twitter: @WordsEnMotion or email wolftracksinwords@gmail.com

© Cari Greywolf Rowan

The Weary Lioness

"Roar!" she told herself.
Self responded, "I can't.
There's a hole in my core."

She slithered into a ball
onto the cold stone floor,
comforted by the hardness.

Desolation held her tightly.
No fight left, she surrendered,
broken finally and on her own.

"Whatever happened to me?"
she wept half-heartedly
because half a heart is all that remained.

She lay slowly deteriorating,
cells rupturing, muscles
torn asunder, the center gone.

"Roar!" her soul demanded.
"Where there's a will,
there's an awakening."

She lay on the hard cold stone,
acknowledging the words,
praying for strength to respond.

Welcoming

Lying naked on the ground
listening to the sounds of night,
rain washing away my tears
I sink into the earth, allowing
her field to embrace me,
enfolding me with love,
reminding me there's a solid core.

Fragile & tender & strong & more resilient than realized,
we take a breath at a time,
together reaching out
across the distances, to remind us
we are not alone. Searching the eyes
of strangers for the look that
says, "Oh, you, too!"

Remembering the essence of love,
the innocence of joy, the laughter of a child,
the gentle touch of our beloved,
the sunrise on Maui, the triple
rainbows in Wyoming, the feel of
morning dew on bare feet,
the aspen's gold in autumn,
the lyrics of a favorite song,
the last time we danced,
a ripe tomato ready to be plucked,
mother tucking us into bed,
her gentle kiss on our foreheads,
a good book in our hands,
a meal shared with friends.

Grace descends, a gift arising from
the ground, falling from the skies,
recalling me from my recoil.
Remain open, especially when it hurts

The Aging of Love

In the early days of love,
I would watch you sleep.
Beauty at peace,
'til I grew sleepy.
Then, gently reaching
to barely touch the ends
of your long hair, the slimmest
connection, I'd fall asleep, content.

Years later, when we'd both
been bruised by unmet needs
and too many angry words,
I'd lie quietly next to you,
matching my breath to yours.
With a delicate contact, I'd place
my hand on your back and
send love straight to your heart.

Our love has matured, now tender
as we each meet new limits
brought by aging. We sit on the couch
and hold hands quietly in deep
familiarity as we grow old together.
Through all our ups and downs,
love, our constant northern star.

No Straight Lines in Nature

Military marches
yardsticks
church pews
poured concrete
tall buildings
squat houses
well-organized closets
regimented thinking
neatly aligned rows of desks

Tidy little stackable boxes to hide the messiness inherent in creative life.
Patriarchal attempts to impose man-made limitations on the natural world.
Placing the human mind, heart, and spirit in rigid, square boxes until
it's time to consign the bodies to rectangular coffins, buried in linear holes
until they are recycled back into the welcoming, rounded womb of the earth.

Rather, give me classrooms of circles,
kids splayed out over the floor.
Nurture arcs and circles,
spirals and waves
and vibrating
moonbeams,
shimmering
into earthly shadows.
Lay my corpse in the Earth
naked as I was born, without a single straight
line in this amazing body of waves,
with muscles that spiral,
tendons that twist,
bones that arc.
Unpredictable,
rebelling against
false order rigidly
imposed on breathing life.

Even a bullet arcs in its flight.

No Wrestling, No Angels

How fast do katydids rub their legs together to make that sound?
Why didn't the crows that lived in our yard ever bring me a trinket?
I'd like a token, a small gift of farewell.
What's the average lifespan of a snapping turtle?

Do you think we'll ever colonize the moon?
How long will the earth take to heal from nuclear winter?
What turns people into suicide bombers?
~likely an easier death than watching breath seep slowly away.

What's the largest tomato ever grown?
Can you trust the labels on food? Is organic really organic?
I tried so hard to live a healthy life.
Should I have chosen a more reckless, rebellious path?

Did Jesus really die for their sins?
I'd like a dark and quiet crypt to lie in now.
I wonder~ how much did the Buddha weigh?
Are any of the creation stories true?

How long 'til sunrise? I lie here, awaiting the final exhale.
What difference does it make if I die in the dark?
And why the hell wasn't Warren Zevon
        ever placed in the hall of fame?
Knocking on heaven's door, he continued to make masterful music.

Phil Saltonstall

It was only moments before,
when he was walking the steps of an otherwise comprehensible life,
when a Spielberg thriller-style special effect moment,
known as the novel he was writing,
opened in the reality around him
and began to swirl.
Reflecting on it, there had been signs…
like when Tsunami waters recedes just prior to the wave.
Everything began to characteristically change.
In his case it was an amplification of circumstance that was the whale that
swallowed him….
the seduction of its realness too persuasive to stand separate from.
The writing portal opened…
he dove into a vortex tiled with living images of pungent poignancy.
Everything swirls, and he becomes the center of
an experiential rotoscope.
There was only one way to work with it…
writing was the floatation device in a swirl of continuous synchronicity…
elements beyond counting,
so for one,
he wrote…
… to not drown.

My name is Phil Saltonstall.
I have been a photographer and conceptual illustrator for 30 years.
A subliminal part of me grabbed my inner remote and changed my channel.
I'm still creating pictures, but I've realized I no longer need
a camera or brush.
I have no idea how I got here.

www.philsaltonstall.com

already here

Illustration by Phil Saltonstall www.photo-illustrator.com

death was coming.
the doctor said arrival imminent.
not only had it already left the station
inbound for me,
it had embarked twice,
first long ago
traveling slow and determined,
and again,
a last minute guarantor,
dispatched to arrive at the same time...
duplicate harbinger.

mr healthy vs two unrelated stage 4 cancers
sponsored by
"ChemLife- where anything is possible."
(they got that right.)
and the first of many many many many needles
went into my arm...
as the concept of basic survival
went into ambiguity.

it was from that place
where all that's certain
abandons ship,
and leaves you tied to the mast
of your own trajectory.
the birds circle.
the sun, moon, and utter darkness of death
play with your delirium...
carnivore to prey
carnivore to pray

a nurse in black rubber gloves
squeezes a bag of ice cold poisonous blue gel,
too thick to drip,
into a now bulging vein.
the Elements
sun, moon, and utter darkness of death,
dance as equals,
while my body
succumbs to seize...
eyes rolled back
and lips speak only foam.
a genetically modified syrup
carried upon the hard sacrificed genome
of countless laboratory mice,
burrows deep into every cell
to reconfigure my marrow.

though formlessness beckons,
there's a core part of me that sees absurdness
in the attraction of it's beauty...
timelessness awaits,
it's hand outstretched in warm welcome...
not in the guise of a reaper
but as a release from inconceivable pain.

yet here....
theres no such thing as hurry.
now, is not the time.
now instead becomes Now.
the ghost of Marley calls across the void singing the words,
"...all i ever had"
which becomes truth...
even when forgotten.
I dig deep for the last token of what is left of me
place my bet on Now's number
and spin her myriad wheel.

Elements dance in possibility,
knowing outcome
is to be anything other
than what's been planned.
the only certainty
is that Their dance,
and the way they move within it...
is life itself.

enthralled as witness,
captivated as partner,
we dance together
to breathlessness.
I shed my indifference.
I find the matter...
and as heaven opens her gates
and I look out from inside...
already here.

you finally wrote...

You finally wrote.
after six months of checking my phone dawn to dusk,
and more pathetically,
in the restlessness of tussled nights turned blue in hope of an opening.
"Don't ever contact me again"
was the jagged edge you used to sever me.
So I waited, gave up, waited, lost hope, waited more, and finally
gave up
yesterday
you wrote to me
after multiple refills of ativan,
obtained by unleashing crippling grief
in the pallor of fluorescent grey at a doctor's office, wet in
embarrassment.
I couldn't hold my shit together when the life i'd survived cancer for,
was stolen by the pick pocket of your insidious fear...
and dumped in an unmapped alley of utter indifference
from which there was no no way out until
yesterday,
you wrote to me
within seconds of my completing a poem
born from purging a need for you to accept me for who I am...
the person you never knew...
beautiful, loving, genuine.
I let you go in front of 900 people
to cement into place this monumental change.
I willed myself to kill the yearning I had seduced myself to sleep with,
abandoning that clamor for mercy...
a tactic learned from you.
Writing you into oblivion gave life
to a newly found sense of relief I hadn't felt till
yesterday,
you wrote to me,
inviting me to meet you at a cafe an hour from now
after six months of my flailing
for the never-to-be-reached rungs of the ladder
that lead the way out of the rabbit hole of pathetic misery.

While you were waiting at a table in a cafe we used to frequent,
I was summoning at mine the intuitions that you and I are inextrica-
bly linked,
and tamping their embers
to prevent fires of love from burning me again.
Rustling in the ash,
stirred the enigma of infinite possibility,
unseen for months that had been masquerading as years...
years of despondent days
that craved
for a yesterday
you wrote to me
at the very moment I had tried to let you go.
I stand unveiled in my withdrawal.
Time melts into Now from the heat of a rising phoenix,
carrying aloft the dead dreams of lost aspiration,
and scattering once again,
seeds of knowing...
that we are more than this...
seeds planted long before,
yesterday
you wrote to me.

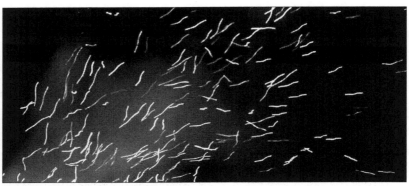

Illustration by Phil Saltonstall www.photo-illustrator.com

Mom's goodbye

She was a lady of finery and manners, and she was dying.
Having lived a life of white gloved soirées and forced etiquette,
for which she would never complain,
she now lay adrift on dank sheets in the humiliation of an incontinence diaper.
Bones that had carried her blithely across stages of life from jumprope to alter,
now fused in an osteoporotic collapse.
She would never get out of this bed alive.
It was nurses never met,
barging in to crush seventy five years of continuous modesty,
that forced her surrender.
"Now I'm gonna roll you over honey, don't you mind".
How could she not mind ?
This was a woman who had been discreetly holding back flatulence
for three quarters of a century, even when no one was in the room.
As kids we had teased her for wasting water as she ran the tap in
the bathroom, lest someone hear her pee.
I realized only now, how mean we were.
She spoke to me in slow motion through the mists of
a morphine cloud,
insisting she was still the twenty two year old Stanford girl
who looked like Grace Kelly's sister,
and I agreed,
she was.
I went outside to reflect, while the nurses attended to business,
and family fragments started to arrive.
Awkward hugs. False kisses that didn't land, floated
over wanting cheeks.
"So great to see you how's she doing flight was terrible".
I walked away thinking about how we were all false kissing,
and we'd all learned from mom.
Some things were just too intimate, and were to be tempered
with appropriate reserve.
The pesky hello/goodbye kiss was always near the top of a long list.
One does their best.
Maybe it was a sanitary issue, like not sharing sips from the same
glass, and not breastfeeding your babies...
All I know is that to this day, I feel uncomfortable with
hello/goodbye kissing, and live with crippling separation anxiety.

I return to her room because I want to hear more of her stories…
The ones that surface when there's only fleeting hours or minutes
for them to be heard.
Their moving her around to change the lowly diaper
has wakened pinched nerves
who now leach pained screams through the cracks
of a crumbling spine.
She doses again, rambles in scat words incoherently,
and returns perhaps, to Stanford.
I sat for hours listening to her barely breathe.
Sudden gasps puncture the calm.
As I get up to leave, I realize that this may be the last time
I will ever see her.
And even with this, I feel too awkward to land a kiss.
so I float away…
in appropriate tempered reserve.

Illustration by Phil Saltonstall www.photo-illustrator.com

notes sympatico

I can hear your heart's call
across a room
of moving static egos.

The noise of your inner voice
now amplified to shrill.
Softness,
and any remaining vestiges,
have been stolen...
and there's no way for you to hear its touch again.

I hear trust being kidnapped, dragged away,
abducted...
made to cry until there's nothing left.
Tears rendered useless,
squeezed from your wounded heart
and collected into a cocktail of conquest,
spiked with the jagged skewers of indifference
and oozing pustules of ego run amuck...
all to then be sloshed upon a wall of somnambular narcissistic
greed...

I hear that your ruminations of a love shared in the sanctity of
sacredness
where divine feminine and divine masculine
balance
in a ballet of archetypal harmony,
have been so ravaged
they hide recoiled...
convulsing in repetitive motion
against the shell walls
of your emotional nautilus.
...its so beautiful btw.

What you once held as the dream come true
of magnetic devotion and mutual connective bliss,
has now been violated out of your loving soul...
You were impaled, literally,
by one who deceived you.
One who knew nothing of sacred spaces,
but lives to pray and prey,
upon those who do.

I hear angels hard at work...
crowding you with seekers
who are drawn to your light.
You, the candle,
appearing as apparition in their individualized darknesses.
Emotional zombies disguising themselves as safe,
who keep coming and coming like they do in the movies...
until you drop to your knees in surrender,
because everybody wants, or needs,
something from you.

I hear you wondering
how anyone might have heard all this...
knowing that the entire tragedy
the mishaps
the putrid mess of it all,
were fish-wrapped in prayers
that only you,
and a universal divine,
might know.

I'll tell you...
there are some who cannot but help to hear
the subsonic pitch of love
when it is laying fallow in despair.
It is the ocean in which they evolved to swim.
You might call them angels,
or just beings who don't know
how not to read signs.
They've been stricken with involuntary literacy
that allows them to see clearly
through the fire of human emotions burning from the inside out in
phosphoric agony.
... more than allows...
Their hearts spill in empathy because their eyes have been sewn open...
and compassion prevents them being able to look away from your pain
and taking it all...
in.

It is from this place
where my heart strings chime
as though strung across the body of an seasoned lute.
They ring true only because notes from yet another seasoned lute
play from across the room...
inviting mine to vibrate untouched, simpatico.
And this remains true,
even if the room,
or a world,
is filled with noise....
for the notes being played,
I know by heart.

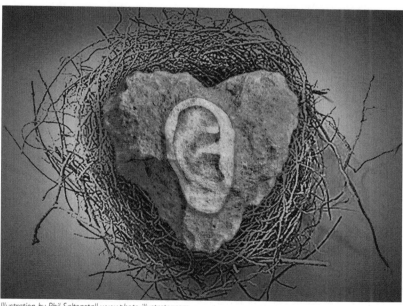

Illustration by Phil Saltonstall www.photo-illustrator.com

Suppleness

a rather courageous woman
found a leather jacket
resting upon the shoulders
of a man who was adept at losing them...
leather jackets, and courageous women.

this very one had been around the length of time
to be at high risk of disappearing...
the jacket....
the woman.
the jacket, because it was now two years worn
and had completed it's journey of attaining a perfect suppleness.
the woman, met two weeks ago that he couldn't stop thinking of.
she subconsciously broadcast thoughts to his once private frequency.
she was probably married, or stuck in something that didn't sustain
or enliven her....
and her thoughts carried across timespace and jacked into him like
a neural implant.

as do the truly homeless ...
she encamped the on barren streets and avenues of her heart...
acrid in loneliness and cold.
despite the hardness and perhaps because of it,
she lived awash in the awareness of her own inherent
suppleness.

he sensed all of this...
it energetically streamed from here silence,
yet her most private thoughts he might never know,
if "life as usual" prevailed in it's lackadaisical way.
mediocrity has an insidious prevalence,
especially when miraculousness is wanting to seep under the door.
in meeting the people you feel,
the trapdoors are often mislabeled by thought and rationale.

in losing all the leather jackets
he had seeded miracles for the finders who happened upon them.
for those chosen few...
touched by the angelic forces embedded in his inherent absent
mindedness,
it was a special day to be remembered...
like when you meet someone new
who ends up in your life...
for life.
we all know those days almost never happen.
...except when they do.

all those old lost jackets
were for others, seeds of new beginning:
the wide lapeled dark brown pawn shop trench coat,
glossed with the ghosts of past pimpitude...
that Joe Strummer jacket with railroad zippers
that he'd sweated through mosh pits of Clash concerts elbows flying,
while pocket contents disappeared into the lining...
and a slick black Versace svelte mid thigh with lambskin grain
softened by european rain and an Italian woman's many embraces...
all waiting to be found
by unsuspecting Rewardians...
people for whom nothing good ever happened...
until it did.

as it does for him...
the loser of jackets,
the finder of a stories awaiting birth.
stories in the on deck circle, like yet-to-be assigned souls...
waiting for divine chance
or a comment from a stranger,
about a jacket that he might be in the process of losing,
that becomes a story about a story
of meeting a courageous woman
who happened to have a soft spot worn from hardness
for noticing...
suppleness.

the untold story of all these jackets,
swirling at the gates of notice,
stopped her long enough
to notice…
his.
the one he was still wearing,
the one that might bring disparate worlds together
or a story of loss,
or ultimate finding.
perhaps to bring into being
someone who might be in your life forever
after decades of seeking through the pits of want…
tenderized by repeated experiences as though meat under mallet.
softening the hide
and where we go to do so.
she says,
"I just love your jacket"

attitudes, thoughts, leather…
everything eventually softens.
perspectives become butter left out of the fridge,
until we put them away again.
the wear and tear of years softens the toughest leather and opinion.
both moistened in the alchemy of tears, rain, wanted and unwanted
sweat.
all pocked by the loss of what matters most
into pocket holes and torn linings of our awareness
as we dance the mosh pits with flailing elbows and loving embrace…
and all inevitably softening
into suppleness.

Illustration by Phil Saltonstall www.photo-illustrator.com

Nancy Shiner

My love of writing began as an attempt to create meaning out of a particularly painful past and I share it today in hopes I might provide a voice for those who search for light amidst their own dark places. My other passions include a new-found love for boxing, watercolor art, two 4-legged felines and my role as auntie to three very special and much-loved nieces and nephews. I have been blessed with three mentors who guide my path and light my way—two who see the "more" of me and the one who carries my heart. These words are for them.

Contact me via email at NShinerWrites@outlook.com

Anorexic Wanting

My skin screams to be touched,
Aches with the wanting of it.
This starving skin of mine begging to be recognized.

In Romania, the orphanages are filled with children who are fed
and clothed yet never held.
At first these squalling infants wail their wanting, desperate for the
feel of human connection.
Yet with time the crying stills as with quiet understanding they
come to know the futility of their yearning.
And unable to receive this most basic of needs, they become passive
in their stillness, a failure to thrive.
"Failure to thrive" a convenient label for children who have never
had the touch of human on their skin.

As for me? I wish to become a Romanian orphan. To have my
neediness turn to numbing so this screaming want will finally cease.
Yet I have no means by which to silence the screaming, thus my
wanting skin begs ceaselessly to be nurtured.

"You must love yourself," the saying goes, but to love a body
unloved is the same as telling a bird with broken wings to fly,
simply because other birds are born with the capacity to do so.
My broken wings grounding me with their impotent flailing.

And how to raise a being into a healthy adult when I'm still a child,
lost inside.
Walking through the world with my raw and oozing skin infected
with the desire to be nurtured.
A woman with no answers. Just questions to be asked and that
constant longing to be held which is far too needy for an adult
who is entering her 46th year.

I am an orphan who never learned to quiet my cravings; thus,
I dream endlessly of gorging on the buffet of stroked skin and arms
encircling that I never knew.
Starving skin, begging to be fed.

Thus I feed on myself. And live constantly hungry.

The Dance of the Ghost Familiar

I feel the return, and it haunts me. The scent of its smoky ash announcing its arrival as it curls into the pit of my stomach and takes residence in the housing it knows so intimately. This old and well-known friend my closest companion.

I breathe in the bloom of its decay as it settles itself into every crack and crevice of the being it's known as home forever. I sigh in relief, in despair, in disgust, as to feel my bones reside in the shadow of this always-known brings its comfort as I know this place so well I feel secure in its haunting. To see its fleeting escape in moments of past brings terror in the loss of a pain familiar, to look in the mirror and find no recognition in the apparition gazing back.

I know my place in the stuckness of its mired encasing. To break my grip from its cement-like stricture a fear of overwhelming proportion that I will lose all self in the face of this unfamiliar embodying. Yet I experience sensation most unusual in the ticklish claw in the back of my throat that begs the question unspeakable.

Who might I be if I wrenched both ankles free from the knuckled grip of the hands that bind me? What face in end might stare with grace from the mirrored walls I hide from? Am I solely the embodiment of the darkness that defines me? Or does possibility exist a new definition for the being I carry so tightly wound could be written on the soul that fights its defining? Questions that rent my apathy in this settling into quicksand of old as they beckon the possibility of something more. A dangerous hope to be sure.

Thus I curl myself into the shadows of familiar and rest my head on its sterile floor. Yet in mind unbidden the spirits are restless, as they stretch legs gone numb from a lifetime unused and consider a dance previously incomprehensible. The dance of a soul being called to life.

And the echo of its drum roll unsettles my troubled sleep.

Feel for Me a Story Child

Tell me how you feel, she whispered.

There is pain behind your eyes suppressed by the film of shame's denial.
Speak your sorrow as it twists and turns within your belly, into something even you no longer recognize.
Spill its inky tenor on the pages of my witness so I may honour the grief that is holding you captive.
For you are human in your grieving.
Made whole in the weeping that breaks free from its caging by a heart grown brittle in its longing.

Release the tethered bonds that bind your numbness and unleash the wailing wall within.
Your throat so tightened by historic stricture, the conviction that emotions' release will split your core and shatter your being.
Thus the words sit unspoken and your cries go unheard and your tears lay unshed, while you suffer the pain of your silence with volcanic eruption of feelings unexpressed.

And you rest in your "Fine" and you drown in your numbness and you seethe in the knowing that your soul has not been recognized.
Yet you have no tools in teaching how to unfurl the raging beast feeding on your innards.

Tell me how you Feel, she said.

In a moment of abandon and with nothing left to lose, I opened up
the floodgates and let spill the tempest storm.
While in the melting of false image and undressing of façade, I
broke free from damning stupor, anaesthesia's deadened stare.
In the face of her calm witness and all absence of denial, I unloosed
my raging fury, 40 years of keening's call.
And the wail that broke the surface of my spirit's dying hull, screamed
the sorrow of a child who'd seen too much and lost her soul.

From the silence of the staircase, behind the locking of the doors, in
the darkness while she shivered, in the hopelessness she bore,
As she begged inside for someone to return and bring her home, till
she learned to kill the longing, stop the wishing to be heard.

I will cry now for her aching. I will rally her defense. I will scream
to flag the footsteps hailing rescue that she sought.
I will weep now for her courage. I will rage her stolen childhood.
I will echo in my sobbing all the innocence she lost.

And through the living of her story, through the telling of her tale,
through the grieving of her passing and annulment of her core,
I will honour all she lived through, this brave warrior of old, and
through my tears that cry a river, sing an anthem to her soul.

Sleep But to Dream of Waking

Sleep, it evades me, like a mist wafting through the room that leaves no trail but the lingering scent of its desire to be captured. The witching hour…and witches indeed.

In the wee hours of the morning my mind brews a poison of bubbling stench; the stink of fear wrapping itself with icy digits around my throat. Evil comes in the night. But morning far worse, as I force myself to put off the dawn in the memory of childhood years when morning brought deliverance to that house of horrors.

Nursery school ran in shifts of morning and noon. I was a morning child year one, by the second I stayed all day, thus alarm clock's toll signalled the inevitable. Mornings enrage me now. When the alarm clock sounds, I am filled with rage before I have even fully sprung to my feet. The desire to take said clock and hurl it through the glass of my window pane almost uncontrollable, while my chest beats the gallop of a horse in full cantor. Hatred and terror intertwine to make me sick with fear.

I hate the hours from nine till noon. Hate them so much that when jobs were an option and I managed to work, I would call in sick time and again, terror so overwhelming I would freeze in my tracks and find myself in retreat to the safety of blankets, shame heavy in the lie that forced my absence.

Years ago, decades even, the solution my brain deciphered was to prevent the dawn from coming at all. As night-time deepens my brain comes alive with thoughts and chaos, constant noise to prevent a resting place that might bring my body to repose. I Google and write, watch nothings on TV, as to focus on even an infomercials' idiocy is far preferable to the relenting of my body to rest.

Days, weeks, months can go by with a body exhausted, sleep taking place between 4 and noon, waking to the reproach of another day wasted. Shame my constant companion for the millions of failures that define my existence. Night, a perfect backdrop for memories' arrival, my desperate fingers searching the Web for the answers to fix the broken me made weaker through my depletion.

Funny the ways a pattern ingrained can direct a path so far off course to redirect becomes nearly impossible. It took years to understand why I hated these mornings. By then the damage done. Forty years of night-time terror makes a habit hard to break, and I sit in the glare of every watt burning and know conquering this fear will be a steep hill to climb.

The nights when my body succumbs to exhaustion and I reluctantly enter the rhythm of sleep, I catapult awake as goblins zippered into men-shaped skins haunt my nightly visions. Then the watch goes on in wait yet again, till morning's rays offer light that signals night's retreat.

There are morning people and night owls or so I've been told, but what if you are neither? Sleep rhythm determined not by melatonin's rise but by the moment in time when a body's hyper-vigilance breaks down sufficiently that it simply ceases to be conscious? Thus I sleepwalk through life, nights lost in chasing answers impossible to find, daytime lost in the fatigue of a body pushed beyond its limit.

"Once upon a time," declares the bedtime story, "there was a little girl." She's haunted now by the lie of happily-ever-after. Big bad wolves and gingerbread witches stealing her happy ending. Praying with the story's final chapter she might write her own "The End", and amend the fable others authored with fairy-tales twisted to suit their own, most evil intentions.

Freedom Day

I am numb these days. Strangely numb and exhausted, yet simultaneously vibrating with unspoken emotion. My soul fights the urge to let down and own its scarlet pain, my fervour frightening in its potential violence.

The tears that gather in the pit of my fog-filled mind scare me with their intensity. The desire to open my lips and let escape the wordless scream that haunts my waking. My teeth the walled off crypt I clench to prevent these zippered lips from offering up their cache. I bite my tongue and leach drops of blood that stain the ground with their longing. I breathe with shallow breath to prevent this furor from stirring in the hollow of my stenotic encasing. Praying for the courage to rent the sheathe from my strictured caging, let loose the stew of pain and rage that threatens to stay my forward motion from finding its progression.

I am a thrashing infant, struggling to birth itself from the shadow of my past with arms and legs flailing, caught mid-labour; unable to push my way through the tunnel of my caging and land blue and breathless to anticipate the rush of air that will pink my waiting cheeks. "Welcome to the world," the cry my longing ears await. My world so habitually constricted to the size of a pinhole that Alice in Wonderland's swallowed libation the fantasized solution to expand body and soul to the fullness of the magnitude it wishes to embody. Yet no Cheshire Cat nor Hatter Mad to direct my path to completion.

I struggle in the prison this numbness engenders; aware emergence to the world requires emancipation of these shackled remnants of old. Yet submission to past indoctrination creates an ingrained instinct to protect myself from possible threat. A prisoner of my own making, the jailers of past having long given over the keys to my ownership.

So I battle the numbness that disguises my longing, fight the paralyzing familiar that prevents my pain from finding escape. Begging the deities of human emotion, should I bow to their greatness I might be delivered from my religiosity of expressions' denial, and given freedom to un-nail both hands and feet from the cross of my daily dying. No longer a slave to the numbness that threatens to assassinate my right to stand present in my fullness.

Thus I walk the line between battlefields of old and today's unknown enfolding. A frightening reality when the cost of reliving history's teachings may result in a complete inability to bloom. Yet unsure whether the bloodshed of feeling's carnage will leave a casualty who walks through the world with permanent wounding. No assurances to be had, though I question every sage that crosses my path in their wisdom.

Hence, I muster my faith and make good my promise to release my self-caging of old. It is time. I no longer have the luxury of freeze or flight. No more the choice to escape the consequence of past misuse. I choose instead to scream out my anguish in the liberation and declaration of my right to my truth.

It's Freedom Day. Today I choose to be free.

Sarah-Alexandra Teodorescu

Sarah-Alexandra Teodorescu was born in Romania, raised in New York and calls Los Angeles home. She lives to love, write, travel, practice and teach yoga, and photograph. She believes in the intrinsic human need to create and connect. Words serve as the bridges across the terrains of her mind and heart. She hopes to leave a comet of inspiration across the horizon of hope.

Follow her in words and photos:
http://lifeisjustastorywritten.com/
Instagram: @lifeisjustastorywritten

I've said goodbye to you a thousand different ways for days upon days upon days. I release you, I release you, I release you. I have sought to pry you from my heart as if I could coerce you from my blood. I have drowned my most precious black-and-white memory in the Ganges. I have buried the remembrance of your voice, and have cast the loving memory of your touch to the wind. I'm watching the sunrise over foreign waters and lands that I have risen in love with, and finally the peaceful moment I have been trying to coax comes. I am alone, but somehow, I summon you by my side. In these moments of beauty and stillness, I resurrect you with poignant clarity. It happens in between the grace and beauty of nature, this ecstatic longing for union. You seem to tilt and shift among the stars, and here in silent reverie, I speak to you. I show you the craters of my heart, always. The memory of you in another life, another place, another face. You turn in slow motion, cast the majesty of your green eyes upon me, and all that I am rests on weary knees, bowed head, tears falling. A relentless love beats itself numb inside of me—if only it could reach you once again, if only you would allow it. The tapestry of remembrance has been has been stitched over lifetimes and is now the chainmail leading me into battle. There is no cave deep enough to contain this love, so it will rise continuously, each time this love taking upon itself a different form. Everything that means something chants softly of everyone you have ever been to me. Always under a different guise, always the same soul, I recognize. There is a part of me that mourns the loss of you eternally. I have learned how to carry it, this separation. I have asked the wisest sentient creatures to show me how, and still, the memory will not fade. Home is a heart we can always invade—the hard-fought grace of remembrance.

I should tell you I love you
Because I whisper it in silence daily.
I worry it will drape on your shoulders like a gift you do not yet
know how to carry.
I will kiss and press into your pained and strained muscles flooded
with memory.
I will do this with absolute tenderness.
You have learned to temper and withstand the blows from others
Handed over under the guise of heartfelt devotion.
You have come to expect them, so the words themselves are the
beginning of the end for you.
I am not like them;
I would not know how to be.
Please, don't fear me.
Three words caught in my heart,
Pleading with all four chambers for an escape route across my lips.
They are burning a trail of vital emotions left unattended in their
silence.
I now know why you feel healed in my presence.
I know why we rest so joyously in each other's embrace.
Love. The word we do not say, but feel building up inside like an
accelerated heartbeat.
This is a gift that must be exchanged
Like an inhale and exhale
From one into the other.

Sometimes, I remember myself and I am indestructible. Other times, you remind me that I am human. Transient. Sentient in an ever changing world. I know that the end result is always far more beautiful than the pain of the sacrifice. It passes through, over and around us. The weaknesses of these minds help us forget, but the strength of the bonds outside of time inflict memories like steel rods anchored through our core. Inescapable. Immortal. This lifetime is just a drop in the oceans of millennia. The memories, piled high like skeletal skyscrapers, built up to be torn down, are found still standing like phantom limbs. And through the mist of forgetfulness, the imprints linger, and though I may never remember your name, I will always feel you real.

I am tired,
But I had to run up here.
As I race myself up
Through the ravines,
I am flooded with an energy
That soars when I am with you.
And now I have a part of you,
Pushing my adrenaline.

In my mind's eye,
I can see
Exactly where I need to go.
I have come to this tree before.
Today, I look up at it
And somehow know exactly what you are.
Ash tree, you reveal yourself to me.
I push my spine alongside your trunk
To steady my heart.
I write out the hardest parts,
The thoughts I know are forming,
The feelings swaying,
My heart chambers once again full.

I close my eyes.
In this moment, the sun and the wind
Kiss my face,
And I remember.
In today's early morning dream,
I understood just how long
We have known each other.
Last night as the flickers of the fire
Illuminated your eyes,
I was reminded that love is
Remembering.

I remember you.
I love you.
I always have.

Not so long ago
That we do not remember still
We were warriors made of light
Warriors before there was a thing called time
By our swords and through our words
Shadows would falter
And fall apart

Not so long ago that we do not remember
We were strong
We were young
Young souls
We shone brightly
Through the void
And inside the silence of space
We were born into stars
And our light
It still reaches you
It lives inside of you

All the beings we have been
All the worlds we have seen
All the knowledge slipping through reality
Escaping from conscious sentient beings

We are the bearers of the world
And all molecules are witnesses
Enchanted by the same stories
Embedded within our DNA
Every atom a piece of the whole

Every living thing has laid claim to its rightful place
inside the city of light
We stand beside you until earth shines encircled in halos
And then she breathes softly
Enshrining everything in immortal white flowers and vines
Until we witness the end of time

Jay Unrau

After decades of dormancy, Jay Unrau has returned to writing due to great online cultural influence. Living in a semi-desolate part of the world with social influences nearby not lending toward support in the arts, Jay factors in his life history and attempts to create a touchable poem or story that will impact any reader.

He is currently working on a collection of poetry and various novels.

"There are no words to describe the imagination, it is the purest gift a human being can possess. Sprinkled with the non-fiction of our experience is where our art begins to take shape."— J.U.

The poetry and prose forwarded to this anthology are a mixture of memories and words that could not be found many years ago, a collection of splinters pulled out too many years later.

Jay can be found on his facebook page – Sla til meg: www.facebook.com/Sla-til-meg-1101508123245698

Hopefully when he finds time, Jay will actually learn how to find a larger audience.

Today

There's a thud today
As my life flashes before my eyes
Slowly.
Then, realizing all was for naught,
Perspective granted.
Salutations as those meant to be
On this road acknowledged
My tires slowing,
Pulling to the side of the road,
Steering wheel thumping,
Inner screams resonating silently
Throughout memorabilia radio songs.
Capturing all my attention:
The faint recall of this life's invention
Poorly planned,
Notes written on my arms,
Stumbling life,
Running when I could barely stand,
Grasping not at treasures wanted,
Memories had
Later haunted,
Full purse of valueless gems,
Decades committed.
When the specter shook his head,
It had been hinted
That wasted days
With passionate beating
Won't satisfy
An always passionate heart.

Not to be mistaken
For sex and disrespect,
It's about breathing quickly.
As you run,
Seek, play with others, laugh,
Discover new worlds.
Hidden amongst them
Is supposed to be you.
Digging deeper.
The hole slowly caves,
Soft sand and wet mud,
The stench of decay ...
Soon the shovel is lost
As you fight to remain
At the top of your memories
Accompanied by faith,
Which slowly departs,
Hope soon to fade
As slowly we arrive
At the day
That's today.
Eyes rolling upwards,
Searching for the spot
Where paths poorly chosen
Deflected your way.
Sitting here truthful to self,
To confess your life in ruins,
Today's been a mess.

Saying Goodbye, Liz-Beth

I prefer the morning light when dew crawls away into the dying of the night.

Into this drying land, we adventured. I was wide-eyed and attentive, searching for youthful clues of a time I faced alone the natural enemies made mostly from my imagination.

We walked down the old road that faltered, almost disappeared amongst the advancing grasses. These paths that a hundred years ago brought settlers north, twisting around long-dried-up creeks, through overgrown poplars and berry patches now starved of sunlight, netting few succulent berries. Waiting fingers, decades from now, will pluck fruit of these bushes in an ecotone far away, in another's time, feasting on full branches of harvest. The past and the future held in one glance, vividly described to my daughter as we travelled past.

I told tales, pointing to each tiny perch. Granaries that hid within the trees, perfect hiding spots for a much-younger me. Cars now abandoned in the shrubs, dying silently, disrespectfully, considering the happy stories they could tell that hesitated on my lips.

She may have thought me too passionate. Childish? Reminiscing creates stuttered memories of childhood that can't take you back. Lived only by one person, not being explained to anyone with the same ease it was lived. Younger legs deserved more time to play. All those years ago nothing was said, except in my mind as I played aimlessly from one side to the other, on the land my grandparents owned, fearing only the unknown or the future.

Glimpses of reality slipped past as bears, deer, and other animals played nearby.

I voiced all that with minute tears in my eyes. Waves of emotions broke my stride. I wasn't even two hundred yards from the house when I saw Caragana Arborescens, planted in my youth, reaching toward the sky, arms outstretched with useless leaves and branches. Once perfect for childhood swords, today merely a giant weed.

We stopped at the old fence posts, emerging from new forest growth just off the road. Decaying, not growing. The Tamarac posts were resilient, and decades later sprouted leaves due to poor trimming of its bark. Or it could have been the vines of the willow growing nearby, taking over the old pasture within that so long ago died. I pointed into the forest that used to house an aging mare and her foals, now just filling with maturing balsams and their cracking bark. I showed her how the dust protects the tree, swiping my hand over once, then blowing gently into the sun.

We followed the solemn trail between the bent trees where meadows ripe for tiger lilies appeared so randomly one had to search for the next. As infrequent as they were, part of my soul was enriched at each surprise sighting.

I had walked, sprinted, and motored down this path so many times. This day's stumbling was unfamiliar. The road had changed as puddles merged over the years under my uncle's tractors. Even with the newer-age equipment, he was careful to leave the settler's trail visible, not barging through with overpowered machinery, giving some reflection to the past and future. Grateful to have permission for my daughter and me, we continued quietly on as light lost the battle to the evergreen's canopy.

These moments filled with chatter moved ahead. We arrived where my parent's and our ancestors' ashes were spread. I shared a tale about each, thoughtful to not favor one over the other. My eyes welled with each emotional story, proudly stating her grandparent's strengths.

With my daughter in my arms, I kept talking until only the hidden stories of our family's personal demons remained—tales not to be told to children. Every family has them. They are the scratches in our metaphorical furniture that cannot be removed, soon become permanent, and are never discussed.

I picked her up and held her to the sun, which fought through the green wings of spruce trees, trying to take flight yet still held firmly rooted to the moist muskeg. We settled to the ground, to wait for the next wind to try again. And although I couldn't look into her eyes, I held the vase as if she were alive, running with me through my wild youth, screaming made-up names into approaching storms; days when I hadn't known that pain is real, before the weight of a heart could drop me to my knees.

As much as I wanted to grasp her and run away, I opened her urn and fed her to the breeze.

I pictured her talking with our ancestors, having just only met her then and there! Alone in my forest. Trod on by my deer. Blanketed with snow each winter. One day to become part of my tiger lilies.

As I tapped the urn against the soft log, afraid I would leave something important inside, I imagined she was running and playing with me, hiding in the trees to play make believe.

The Reason

I cannot find a home

This crosses my mind
Sitting in another group of walls
That do not call my name

Longing to rid myself
Of all collected bobbles
That whisper others' names
And hang onto half-filled diaries
That mumble my own

To once again
Fit everything I own into a rucksack
Pockets bulging with items
To trade along the way
For memories and sunsets

I am not afraid to walk into the shadows
Fill my soul with an unknown harvest
Traipse among the corpses
Of this damaged world

Meeting people who
Having found their huckleberry
Or a rock to call home
Shake a hand and join their fire

But long

For that instance
As my eyes take hold
Of that place or person
I have never seen or met

Whether in a soft lit corner
A fiery battleground
My heart will feel its matching beat
Of a love that is not yet known

Poet's Corner

The drunk writers crossed their pens,
Witnessing verbs, adjectives, and misunderstandings.
Deep within the bar,
Others were just writing,
Furrowed brows,
Reddened cheeks,
Sipping gin and tonic to fuel a madness brewing inside.
That is how we roll,
Each journal uniquely bound,
Audible sounds of tapping pens

While a not-so-gentle voice described
The terrible sins spoken aloud,
Unwinding fictional drama.
After the poems were unveiled,
Creating a stir,
Drunkenness claimed the day.
The poets felt passion

Ownership,
Held the mortgage papers
To the perfect poem
Spoken out loud today.

In the back of the room,
A solitary pen continued to fracture paper as it crossed
Carvings in the soft wood table,
Surrounded by books ne'er dusted,
Chairs becoming musty.
A poet, recognizing the end of the world,
Scribbled as fast as he could,

Writing words to fix it all.
Before he could finish,
Before he could read,
All the poets had left the bar,
Scurried up the darkened exit to a half-lit street,
Rain trickling down onto antique
Oxford shoes, escaping nothing
But their own passion.

"Same time next week,"
Shouted the homeless man
Who was always invited, and bought beer,
For he, too, was a poet,
And belonged here.
Yes, they all agreed,
Escaping into the night.

Over a hush in traffic,
As the street lamps brightened,

We might have heard the perfect poem
Whispered in the empty poet's parlor,
Tucked way behind the bar,
While unpoetic people gathered,
Undeserving,
Hugging the bar meters away.

What the Shade Won't Hide

There is a village in central Africa whose town center is marked with roots of a tree pulled the few miles from the Gishwati Forest. So gnarled are the roots no use could be found for the remnant of a once majestic tree, and to this day, the giant root stands as tall as a man. With the complicated matrix of a tumbleweed, it became the town center, too heavy to blow away as it slowly sinks into the sand beneath.

I arrived as a visitor, politely standing on the outskirts of the village, huts around me made from crude bark and sticks. Woven saplings or branches held everything in place, giving them an unseen strength. Rudimentary baskets were stacked next to doors. Faces, with colorful clothing below, peeked from behind the shade of the day. Hands beckoned me into the village with the casual motion of practised midday relaxation.

Well into the village, I paused at the twisted roots. I looked skeptically into the hundreds of wooden fingers curling back into a ball. I raised an eyebrow, wondering if it was art, or nature imitating art. My local contact appeared at my side, one hand patting the roots and the other pointing to the nearby Gishwati Forest. Within the few words I understood, Macaranga was repeated a few times. As he imitated the dragging motions of the Macaranga trees' journey to the village, I pictured the village men, pulling an old tree hundreds of feet then resting in its still-alive shade.

Over the next weeks, I found this was the way most things were accomplished. With the exception of hot days, which occupied every day of the calendar, something was always happening. Men, women, and children created necessities, toys, and food out of the invisible resources hidden nearby.

Our only task was to create a well in over a hundred villages. Some, like this one in Northwest Rwanda, did not require a well. They were situated near a forest and did not appear to be struggling. Smiles and laughter were only interrupted by the need to rest in the first shade available.

Over the course of weeks of planning, locating water, rounding up the crude materials required to top the wells taps and handles, a mood of uneasiness invaded this normal behaviour. Our Land Rover's purring engines did seem to help for a short period. As the missionaries volunteering to help slowly came and went, so too did the furrows on each local's face.

Buto, my new friend, surrounded by his wife and children, constantly waved down my concerns over his apparent state of alarm. He would point out the forest as if it would solve any undiscussed problem.

"Hiding in the roots?" I would joke lightly.

His eyes were fierce slits of surprisingly brilliant determination, reflections of his personal assurance given to every member of his village.

As the water well unceremoniously progressed over the week, there were many hours spent in the shade, watching the children with homemade bobbles and toys. The women of the village knit fibre to clothing, dyed into miraculous colours, forming gowns that could be sold around the world—if indeed the world knew they existed.

I was not pretentious in the gatherings. I sat and listened, answered if called upon by Buto or the missionaries carrying buckets of mud a short distance away. The mud hardened leaving a grotesque statue. Few of the part-time missionaries noticed the shade, their pale skin reddened. Fatigue sent them to bed under tarps stretched across vehicles.

Eventually, there was a water geyser and cheers from the faithful Christians.

Hours later—when an amateur plumber had tightened all the valves, tested the flow of water and all had gathered for a quick prayer around the donated piping—there was a flurry of biblical propaganda handed out with Crayons and scribblers, followed by the hymn-singing departure of our caravan.

I let Buto know I would be back in the following weeks.

"When?" He asked seriously, repeatedly.

I could not give an exact date. It all depended on politics. Warnings had been arriving daily via phone calls from home. They weren't saying what the troubles were, just saying that coming home was one of the best options.

"Once a week," I stated.

"Seven days from today." His handshake loosened.

"And the same until I cannot." His smile smoothed his wrinkled forehead. That, to Buto, was a relief.

It was a relief to travel without the missionary group, journeys preplanned with an end I did not recognize. All I had known for years was trading, buying, and begging permission for access to drill wells. Constant dusty skin baked to within an hour of well done. My collection of Land Rovers packed with the I-may-need and the just-in-case supplies, my wrapped Kalashnikov, and the satchel of shells protecting Christians from unseen wild animals.

Each morning, each week, it would take a few minutes to start my day. Living in a land that cannot be understood was like a full-time acting career. Preparation included. With those types of days all too common, the trip back to the Gishwati Forest was welcomed.

"Home for Christmas" tingles would invade my often unemotional, serious character. Smiles volunteered themselves as Buto met my truck, guiding it to the center of the village each visit. The more I visited, the more children danced in the rooted village center.

On my last visit, I could tell from a mile away an emptiness awaited. Where fabric would once blow in the wind, only swirls of dust could be seen. By the time the truck sat idling near the village center, Buto could be seen rounding the corner of the nearest hut. Mid-day shades sat empty. Upturned baskets were scattered randomly as if a great wind had just passed through.

"Welcome, Welcome," Buto formally stated, big eyes searching the road I had traveled. Each moment we talked an anxious child or their mother appeared in the shadows. Bundles that normally filled huts were strapped to backs. Babies normally playing with beads spread around blankets were strapped to each woman's chest.

The mood was tense. Having heard of massacres taken place days ago, I did not want to give false hope.

Around the country killing of this people had unofficially started. The Hutus were practising, playing their odds. Not selectively. Geographically killing who was next on the road. This village, on a busy roadway, would have many travelers.

As the evening began, women waved over their shoulders, disappearing into the foliage. Men, with a final look to the southern horizon, disappeared quietly into the night.

I calmly locked my doors and fell anxiously asleep behind the driver's seat. Assuring myself that all would pass quietly, a prayer may have crossed my lips for the first time in decades.

In the last hour of the day, a Red Cross truck—engine steaming—limped through town and seeing no one, left before a door could be opened. Nervous faces with tense white lips stared back at my lone vehicle. Neither stopping, nor wanting to stop.

I awoke to the constant wails, then screams. At first, I tried to wash the dreams out of my ears, hoping remnants remained. As my body accepted the reality, it remained motionless, frozen in what would be remembered for years as too long.

The screams intensified, propelling me upright—one hand holding an already loaded rifle, the other a satchel of shells. I raced towards the forest a mile away, skirting low foliage until it only hindered my progress, then moving without hesitation as I bolted through the waist high shrubs to the edge of the great forest.

Before I could choose my next path, I heard her screams—felt them. Then I saw Buto's wife on her knees, unmistakable bright dress against the moonlit foliage. Her hair was gathered in a man's fist, pulling her away, her arms struggling to free herself, lower body struggling to reach another figure partly hidden ten feet away. My eyes refused to understand what was happening when the devil himself looked at me, then towards the bushes. With a nod and a smile only the Devil himself could wear, the blades raised above the leaves, gleaming as if the sun itself was shining on this night, and fell quickly with tightly-gripped handles. Each arcing stroke ending with the sickening sound of meat separating from bones as her child was skewered, again and again. They had fallen one by one to the ground and now lay motionless near her clawing legs. Her screams rose with each blow, blood trickling down her neck as she tried to separate herself from her scalp.

The last blows fell, and Buto's wife was thrown across the bodies of her children to meet the same fate. As the arm of a man rose to the sky, gleaming machete arcing widely, a shot could be heard.

And then another.

On that day seventeen men were killed. Each of them having no right to live in this world again.

Seventeen!

I would have killed more, but there were only 17 shells.

That night ended, and in the days to follow, I carried bodies to the Gishwati forest, pieces of bodies. One by one. We buried or burned remnants. Ruguru people were buried near the great roots, and the murderers burnt until only ashes remained.

Buto was buried deep at the base of an ancient tree stump. From there he could see the village. His people. From his final resting place, bright eyes could oversee family laid beside him, or those still alive.

Still caked in blood, I left the village, boarded a plane home. Not sure what or why this happened. Ever.

I have heard missionary stories of a village near the Gishwati Forest. In this village is a dead or dying tree with a bell hanging at its center. Each year, on a certain day, the bell is struck 35 times. One for each man, woman, or child lost. After a pause, it is struck again. A single toll for the man that brought water and stayed for one more day.

Darlene Versak

Darlene Versak lives in Plymouth Meeting, PA with her two sons where she finds laughter at the most inappropriate time and in all things, especially herself. Searching for her tribe and living with a heart that has been broken open, she is growing on a daily basis believing that writing her truth will heal her and maybe the world. She works as an accountant, and in the mornings she writes. She has published articles online at Rebelle Society, The Tattooed Buddha and Elephant Journal. She is currently working on her first book.

Facebook: www.facebook.com/LifeAlchemist
Email: lifealchemist333@gmail.com

Darlene Versak ©2016

The Girl the Universe Forgot

Have I been forgotten?
My dream, that is.
Did my bag of want, longing, and love
Get left at the gate?
No one gathered my wishes.
They weren't stored properly—
Jostled about and
Thrown out,
Hurtling head forward
To the ground.

Or,

Were they never heard?
Missed among the litany
Of other's dreams
Deemed more important,
Silenced by the shouts
Of louder voices.

Or,

Did an angel
Drop them?
My dreams simply
Spilling over the top
Or falling through cracks,
Slipping through fingers ...
A feather
Falling silently to the ground.

Or,

Were they simply
Forgotten
In the busyness of the world,
In the breakneck speed of
Moving forward?
The quiet whispers
Of "me, please"
Lost
Or forgotten ...
Except,
By Me.

Upside Down

Driving over the bridge
On a busy two-lane highway,
I should be paying attention.
Cars pass with killing velocity,
But I'm trancing,
Lost in the clouds to my left.

They look like sand that waves have carved into the sky,
Soft and powdery,
With lines divvying them up.
It's as if water has poured through them
To dig channels of blue.

My gaze wanders forward, and I see it—
The part of the sky that is the ocean,
Clear and open,
With wisps of clouds, tossed here and there,
White caps swirling on the sea.
The sun shines through here.

I wonder,
How did the world
Turn upside down?

The Light Within

Yellow sun
Burning bright within my heart
The light within
Clears the darkness

Seeking
Yearning
Being

Grounded in eternity
Floating through time
Release me from the prison
Of supposed to be
Grant me what is true

See through
The walls
The lies
False Gods
To
Truth
Beauty
Love

When Whimsy Won the Day

She came in through my bedroom window.
At least, that's what I think.
A pixie-powder trail at night,
She wanted a quick drink.

The moonstone caught her eye,
The way it plays with light.
A quick detour to whet her smile
And carry on mischief at night.

I followed glitter down the stairs
To where I keep the good stuff.
Pantry doors wide open,
She found her way to enough.

She kicked an expensive red.
I knew she had some taste.
An empty bottle on the table,
Not a drop left to waste.

An ornate note hung above the glass,
Suspended, glowing midair.
"Never give up."
Mouth agape, all I could do was stare.

I heard a giggle, and I knew
As the note—Poof—simply vanished.
My friend was still there,
Watching me survey the damage.

I smiled and said thank you
For words of wisdom given.
Swoosh—the air fluttered,
And I hoped that I would listen.

The glitter faded as dawn appeared.
No proof exists of the visit.
An empty vessel evidence alone
Of this occurrence of kismet.

"No one will believe me,"
I ponder out loud,
"That magic came to play,
Delivering the message found."

I believe in the unknown.
When asked I always say,
"She drank my wine and laughed at me
When whimsy won the day."

Stardust and a Fable

There is stardust in my eyes. If you look closely, you'll see the tiny points of light dancing in the blue. We are all stardust, made from the same elements as the stars. Stardust is like the seeds of the universe planted everywhere. Some seeds are nothing to look at on the surface—take a zinnia seed, for instance. It's teeny tiny and could be lost or passed over very easily. However, plant that seed in fertile soil, nourish it, water it, love it, and it grows into a huge, wild, crazy flower, bending in all directions to reach the light. In many ways, aren't people the same?

When I think of stardust, I think of magic. I think of wands filled with light and enchantment. I think of blinding goodness bewitching all who fall under its spell. We all have the ability to exude light, goodness and most of all love. We are stardust, so why do we settle for so much less?

As children, the world is full of hope, possibilities, and the belief that we can do and be whatever we want. What happens to us? Look into the eyes of a child and see the stardust that lives there. It's in their hopeful gaze that seems to ask "Will you love me?" Something happens along the way, though. We harden. We close doors. We lose our belief that what we want is possible. Our hopeful gaze changes as we question whether we are worthy of love.

The world needs more magic and play. I'm not saying chuck responsibility out the window. I'm saying acknowledge that we are ALL special. We are all stardust.

Yes, I was formed in the heart of a star, and you know what? So were you. When I let that truth settle into my soul, it makes me tingle with excitement. I am magic. This truth makes me feel invincible. Stardust doesn't destruct; it just changes form.

And I can't help but wonder if life were a fable, maybe it would go something like this ...

Once upon a time, there was a girl in a flower dress, living in an enchanted land—a land filled with stardust. It existed in every living creature of this kingdom, but a wicked witch had cast a spell that dulled the inhabitants of this utopia.

At the age of 10, slowly, mysteriously every child would stop believing they were magical. Each day moving forward until the age of 25 (give or take a few years), the people lost the ability to see the magic that existed in and around them. Responsibility and order were what the witch wanted—and control, most of all control.

"We can't have people being wild and all about love. Nothing important will ever get done. People must be kept busy, so they have no time to be magical." The witch said, wanting to control all of the magic herself.

The spell didn't work on everyone. A few rogue magicians existed who wrote songs, books, and painted beautiful pictures, whose lives were truly a work of art. Some people were entranced by the spell for years until it finally began to wear thin, and they slowly awakened and rediscovered their magic.

The girl in the flower dress woke up after many years of slumber and decided the best way to fight the witch was to dance in the public square, hand out flowers, and shower everyone she met with love. She told everyone about the magic they possessed—her mission to wake up all she encountered in the hopes they would, in turn, wake up everyone they encountered.

It took some time, but eventually, the scale tipped. The number of awake people outnumbered the numb people, and the spell faded into the background. Most of the enchanted land woke up; however, there were a few loyal to the witch who staunchly refused to see their own magic.

The kingdom was changing, though, and almost everyone lived knowing they were stardust and capable of anything. The world was happier for it.

Becca West

Becca West is an artist and writer living in Oklahoma City. She has work appearing across the city from the side of buildings to chalkboards and t-shirts. When she isn't behind a paint brush or pencil, you can find her being pulled by her four dogs, Ringo, Lloyd, Puppy, and Han Solo. Though she didn't pursue art until college, Becca has been writing since a young age and has had a few poems published in anthologies before. If you wish to find more of her strange life, check out www.bwsquared.com.

Speeding

When it's dark and high beams are on,
I always think back to when Dad taught me how to drive
In a parking lot
Small circles
Parking
Reversing
Turning

If I crossed over a line I wasn't supposed to

He'd say something along the lines of

    Oh, you just hit a cat

Or

    There goes a puppy

And I would laugh like I was supposed to
But deep down
It hurt because
I knew how dangerous this really was
I knew that this was steel and speed and responsibility
And I didn't know if I was ready

He taught me

How to watch the white line
Where to position on the hood
So I'd always be in the lines
A form of fast paced coloring

How to watch when it's dark
For the beams of others
So I could turn mine off out of courtesy
That bored cops
Were always running plates
In the early mornings of their shifts
And most people talk their way into tickets

Every time I get behind the wheel I think of where to put my hands
How intimidating this once was
Now is as easy as breathing
I think about Dad
How he taught me how to drive
But when he drove
He was always speeding

Burn

I like the way the lighter feels in my hand

With a small flick of the thumb
And a spark of imagination
I watch this whole town burn
It
In itself
Is just a small cylinder of plastic
Yellow with white polka dots
I picked up in desperation
At a gas station

The old beard behind the counter
Questioning my motives
And I just smiled
Dropped a five
And walked out

Remember when you were a kid
Playing with candles
Seeing who could hold their finger in the yellow the longest
I always failed
Too scared to get burned
Too scared of losing
I didn't even try
And I watched in wonder as the bravest pinched out the flame
Like it was nothing

I like the way the lighter feels in my hand

Control
And heat
And fear worth conquering

Everything

He wasn't my dream
My dream was barefoot
Adventures
It was Italian
Museums
Long hair
Flowing out the window on cross country road trips

Cozy nights
Pen in hand in some anywhere place
My dream wasn't a wistful prince
That whisks the damsel out of danger
It was more like
Robin Hood
Running through the trees
Laughing at my own conquests

He knew he wasn't my dream
As I knew I wasn't his

I wasn't the cleanly wife
Who couldn't wait for little ones
I didn't want to stay home waiting
While he worked hard for our money
I didn't need to be pampered
Or put together
I was restless and messy
And most of the time
His own personal smiling disaster

And he would shake his head
Throw his hands up
Smirking
What am I going to do with you
And I would reply
Everything

Away

I didn't bury you
I couldn't bear the thought of them lowering you into the ground
I couldn't stand above
First fist full of dirt
While everyone's tears fed the February grass
I couldn't give your death a place
Or I would have curled up like a fox in winter
Begging them to bury me too

No

Instead I chose the fire
And the pastor told me of the early Christians
Of the second coming
The idea that our bodies must be intact
But I didn't understand
Wasn't it from dust to dust
I chose the fire for you

Ironic

The little boy that snuck matches
Setting his mother's flowers on fire
And the grown man I found
Digging a fire pit in the middle of our rented backyard
And the tobacco pipe you would puff on
Coming to bed smelling of sweet evening smoke

But

When your dad handed me the heavy
Blue velvet box saying

> My son
> My poor son
> In such a small container

I knew I would carry you
Until the wind blew us both away

Vesuvio, San Francisco

I could be anywhere
Deep Dark Bar
Hazy lamp light
Beer sloshing in my shoes

I could be anywhere
Yellow taxi cabs
Neon lights
Chatter streaming through open doors

I could be anywhere
But
I am here

Two men and a Gloria pen in hand
Stories shared out of thin air
Out of places normally hid in closets
Stuffed in shoe boxes on the top dusty shelf
But not here

Not just anywhere
Which is where I could be

But here
Beer in my shoes
Words scattered over me
Table cracker crumbs of our lives
Have there ever been stranger mice than these

Index of Authors

Index of First Lines

Acknowledgments

Writing is an act of creation the second a thought reaches our fingertips with rushes of imagination, emotion, and moments of doubt. Words tumble to the canvas of bound journals, lined paper, napkins, or screens. It is a skeletal, shimmering, tranquil vision that's birthed—sometimes gasping for its life, always begging to be held.

Without the familial bond discovered quite by accident during the last year, this project would not have found its way to your hands. What was once a solitary endeavor became a collective breathing of words onto the pages of this anthology. Dreamed of, carried, and finally in the last stretch of cooperation, perfected by contributing writers, editors, marketers, and artists. It is as much a reflection of friendship as it is artistry.

Jen Pope took her faith in our words, believing "if you build it, they will come." She sent out the call for our best work, and with pen and paper in hand, we arrived. She slipped notes under the door, continuing to express her belief and confidence as we moved forward on this journey.

Joseph Kittilson, hearing Jen's initial vision, grounded it with further wisdom. "First you find a place to till the soil," he said. Together, they created a safe space in which the authors could share concerns or inspiration, urge each other along, and speak our thoughts unjudged. Joseph has been the quiet one behind the scenes—motivating, soothing, urging us forward, that firm hand on the shoulder when needed most.

Gary Gregory has played many roles in the achievement of our goal—his presence threaded throughout the process. Equally skilled in writing and knowledge of marketing, publicity and the route to publication, our words might have no ears to hear if his talent and willingness to do the hard work of connecting us to our audience had not been undertaken.

All this would have been for naught if we hadn't found the messages we wanted to share. Once we did, we turned to our friends to edit, and at times, allow that first breath to happen. Our craft is personal, protected, and for many sacred, so the process of editing our words does not come easily. In fellow writers, we found those who cared about our voice more than syntax, and although these wordsmiths often work in the shadows, they found ways to empower each writer to add a shimmer or shadow if needed or raise their voices when required.

Without the considerable time and effort of Melissa Kuchel, many of us may have exited this project with unpolished chapters or efforts that did not reflect the best we had to offer. Melissa treated our words with utmost respect and dignity as she gently coaxed each tiny improvement, allowing each writer's voice to simply speak with clarity.

Cari Greywolf spent time in quiet reflection in nature and the woods she loves, realizing that "in sharing our words, others breathed them in." In that breath, we found our title. This was not her only contribution. Cari acted as both coach and champion for each piece she edited, and our words, in the end, were the better for her gentle consideration.

Our words now ready, Leslie Bolin took over, working tirelessly behind the scenes, compiling and formatting each draft of our manuscript. She has remained unfailingly patient with our last minute revisions, the author's ever-changing deadlines, and faithful to the intention to create a book that would reflect the final vision we each imagined.

Phil Saltonstall took the gift of our words and wrapped them with skill, forethought, and ability, creating a book cover that conveys countless thoughts, words, and intensely personal revelations in an image that speaks the story of our collective heart. Two profiles exhaling their words into the ether speaks passionately to those who entrusted him with this task and reveals his deep understanding of our desire to use our words to connect with the greater world.

We are grateful to Tyler Knott Gregson, published poet, author and professional photographer, who saw the manuscript before publication, and extended valuable words of encouragement.

This group of writers and contributors have beat impossible odds and worked together to create a book reflective of this rare collaboration. We are proud of one another, deeply moved by the gentle proddings and encouragement that allowed our words to breathe. We are grateful for the opportunity to share them with you.